S0-BDL-379

Michael J. Furlong
Gale M. Morrison
Russell Skiba
Dewey G. Cornell
Editors

Issues in School Violence Research

Issues in School Violence Research has been co-published simultaneously as *Journal of School Violence*, Volume 3, Numbers 2/3 2004.

Pre-publication REVIEWS, COMMENTARIES, EVALUATIONS . . .

"**P**ACKED WITH INFORMATION and insight. . . . A QUINTESSENTIAL RESOURCE FOR SCHOLARS, GRADUATE STUDENTS, AND PROFESSIONALS. The nationally recognized experts contributing to this book address a breadth of topics related to school violence, including bullying, high-risk behaviors, warning signs, school climate, discipline, surveying students, and weapons at school. This book provides core knowledge that has numerous implications for professional efforts to prevent violence at school and promote safe, effective, and responsive schools."

Shane R. Jimerson, PhD
Professor of Child and Adolescent Development and Professor of Counseling, Clinical, and School Psychology, University of California, Santa Barbara

More pre-publication
REVIEWS, COMMENTARIES, EVALUATIONS . . .

"SHINES MUCH-NEEDED LIGHT ON WEAK METHODOLOGIES AND OUTDATED PROCEDURES. . . . Elucidates important new directions for advancing research quality and understanding. . . . Critically examines the uses of self-report bullying surveys, office referrals, and traditional, criminal behavior-influenced school safety surveys, and OFFERS IMPORTANT INSIGHTS AND RECOMMENDATIONS that administrators and program evaluators will find valuable. The editors have gathered an impressive author group of 'A-list' researchers and theoreticians. The book has been assembled in a manner that speaks informatively to those who would use the research to direct policy and practice as well as the researchers who seek to acquire it. For researchers, comprehensive discussions of methodological pitfalls and intriguing directions for the application of new models make this volume AN ESSENTIAL ADDITION TO ANY PERSONAL LIBRARY."

Jim Larson, PhD
Professor and Coordinator,
School Psychology Program,
University of Wisconsin-Whitewater;
Member, Scientific Board,
The Melissa Institute for Violence
Prevention and Treatment

The Haworth Press, Inc.

More pre-publication
REVIEWS, COMMENTARIES, EVALUATIONS . . .

"**O**F GREAT VALUE. . . . Provides a much-needed focus
on several critical methodological
and measurement issues pertaining to the evaluation of school-
based programs designed to prevent bullying and school violence. Of particular value is an
in-depth examination of the validity and reliability of two popular
measures of bullying and school
violence: student self-reports and
office referrals. Another important issue addressed is the frequent overreliance on measures
of low-incidence behaviors, such
as dangerous behavior and criminal actions, and the neglect of
more frequent behavior problems
and the overall school climate."

George Bear, PhD
*Professor, School of Psychology,
University of Delaware*

The Haworth Press, Inc.

Issues in School Violence Research

Issues in School Violence Research has been co-published simultaneously as *Journal of School Violence*, Volume 3, Numbers 2/3 2004.

Issues in School Violence Research has been co-published simultaneously as *Journal of School Violence,* Volume 3, Numbers 2/3 2004.

© 2004 by The Haworth Press, Inc. All rights reserved. No part of this work may be reproduced or utilized in any form or by any means, electronic or mechanical, including photocopying, microfilm and recording, or by any information storage and retrieval system, without permission in writing from the publisher. Printed in the United States of America.

The development, preparation, and publication of this work has been undertaken with great care. However, the publisher, employees, editors, and agents of The Haworth Press and all imprints of The Haworth Press, Inc., including The Haworth Medical Press® and Pharmaceutical Products Press®, are not responsible for any errors contained herein or for consequences that may ensue from use of materials or information contained in this work. Opinions expressed by the author(s) are not necessarily those of The Haworth Press, Inc. With regard to case studies, identies and circumstances of individuals discussed herein have been changed to protect confidentiality. Any resemblance to actual persons, living or dead is entirely coincidental.

The Haworth Press, Inc., 10 Alice Street, Binghamton, NY 13904-1580 USA

Cover design by Jennifer M. Gaska

Library of Congress Cataloging-in-Publication Data

Issues in school violence research / Michael J. Furlong . . . [et al.] editors.
  p. cm.
  "Co-published simultaneously as Journal of school violence, Volume 3, Numbers 2/3 2004."
  Includes bibliographical references and index.
  ISBN 0-7890-2579-5 (hard cover : alk. paper) – ISBN 0-7890-2580-9 (soft cover : alk. paper)
  1. School violence. I. Furlong, Michael J., 1951- II. Journal of school violence.
LB3013.3.I88 2004
371.7'82–dc22
                             2004014673

Issues in School Violence Research

Michael J. Furlong
Gale M. Morrison
Russell Skiba
Dewey G. Cornell
Editors

Issues in School Violence Research has been co-published simultaneously as *Journal of School Violence*, Volume 3, Numbers 2/3 2004.

The Haworth Press, Inc.

New York • London • Victoria (AU)
www.HaworthPress.com

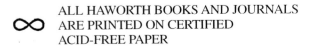

ALL HAWORTH BOOKS AND JOURNALS ARE PRINTED ON CERTIFIED ACID-FREE PAPER

Indexing, Abstracting & Website/Internet Coverage

This section provides you with a list of major indexing & abstracting services. That is to say, each service began covering this periodical during the year noted in the right column. Most Websites which are listed below have indicated that they will either post, disseminate, compile, archive, cite or alert their own Website users with research-based content from this work. (This list is as current as the copyright date of this publication.)

Abstracting, Website/Indexing Coverage . . . . Year When Coverage Began

- *Australian Education Index <http://www.acer.edu.au>* . . . . *

- *Cambridge Scientific Abstracts is a leading publisher of science information in print journals, online databases, CD-ROM and via the Internet <http://www.csa.com>* 2002

- *CINAHL (Cumulative Index to Nursing & Allied Health Literature), in print, EBSCO, and SilverPlatter, Data-Star, and PaperChase. (Support materials include Subject Heading List, Database Search Guide, and instructional video) <http://www.cinahl.com>* . . 2003

- *Contents Pages in Education* 2002

- *Criminal Justice Abstracts* . . . . *

- *Educational Administration Abstracts (EAA)* 2002

- *e-psyche, LLC <http://www.e-psyche.net>* 2002

- *ERIC: Current Index to Journals in Education (CIJE) <http://ericacve.org>* 2003

- *Family Index Database <http://www.familyscholar.com>* 2003

- *Family & Society Studies Worldwide <http://www.nisc.com>* 2002

- *Family Violence & Sexual Assault Bulletin* 2002

(continued)

- *Gay & Lesbian Abstracts provides comprehensive & in-depth coverage of the world's GLBT literature compiled by NISC & published on the Internet & CD-ROM (www.nisc.com). For more details write to: NISC, Wyman Towers, 3100 St. Paul Street, Baltimore, MD 21218 USA. Phone: (+1) (243-0797) FAX: (+1) (410) (243-0982). e-mail: sales@nisc.com. Online: www.nisc.com <http://www.nisc.com>* **2002**

- *Index to Periodical Articles Related to Law <http://www.law.utexas.edu>* . . . . *

- *Injury Prevention Web <http://www.injurypreventionweb.org>* **2002**

- *Linguistics & Language Behavior Abstracts (LLBA) <http://www.csa.com>* **2003**

- *National Clearinghouse on Child Abuse & Neglect Information Documents Database <http://nccanch.acf.hhs.gov>* **2003**

- *Prevention Evaluation Research Registry for Youth (PERRY).* . . . . *

- *ProQuest Research Library. Contents of this publication are indexed and abstracted in the ProQuest Research Library database (includes only abstracts . . . not full-text), available on ProQuest Information & Learning <http://www.proquest.com>* **2004**

- *Referativnyi Zhurnal (Abstracts Journal of the All-Russian Institute of Scientific and Technical Information–in Russian)* . . . **2003**

- *Research into Higher Education Abstracts* **2002**

- *SafetyLit <http://www.safetylit.org>* **2004**

- *Social Services Abstracts <http://www.csa.com>* **2003**

- *Social Work Abstracts <http://www.silverplatter.com/catalog/swab.htm>* **2002**

- *Sociological Abstracts (SA) <http://www.csa.com>* **2003**

- *Violence and Abuse Abstracts: A Review of Current Literature on Interpersonal Violence (VAA)* **2002**

- *Worldwide Political Science Abstracts (formerly: Political Science & Government Abstracts) <http://www.csa.com>* **2003**

*Exact start date to come.

(continued)

Special Bibliographic Notes related to special journal issues (separates) and indexing/abstracting:

- indexing/abstracting services in this list will also cover material in any "separate" that is co-published simultaneously with Haworth's special thematic journal issue or DocuSerial. Indexing/abstracting usually covers material at the article/chapter level.
- monographic co-editions are intended for either non-subscribers or libraries which intend to purchase a second copy for their circulating collections.
- monographic co-editions are reported to all jobbers/wholesalers/approval plans. The source journal is listed as the "series" to assist the prevention of duplicate purchasing in the same manner utilized for books-in-series.
- to facilitate user/access services all indexing/abstracting services are encouraged to utilize the co-indexing entry note indicated at the bottom of the first page of each article/chapter/contribution.
- this is intended to assist a library user of any reference tool (whether print, electronic, online, or CD-ROM) to locate the monographic version if the library has purchased this version but not a subscription to the source journal.
- individual articles/chapters in any Haworth publication are also available through the Haworth Document Delivery Service (HDDS).

ABOUT THE EDITORS

Michael J. Furlong is Program Chair of the Counseling/Clinical/School Psychology Program and Professor in the Gevirtz Graduate School of Education at the University of California, Santa Barbara. He is also Director of the Center for School-Based Youth Development and Associate Editor of *Psychology in the Schools* and the *California School Psychologist*. A past president of the California Association of School Psychologists, his research interests focus on school violence and safety and social and emotional assessment.

Gale M. Morrison is Professor in the Counseling/Clinical/School Psychology Program in the Gevirtz Graduate School of Education at the University of California, Santa Barbara. Her research interests have included social/emotional adjustment of students at risk for learning and behavior problems, parent/professional relationships, and the role of support services to the education mission in the schools. Her focus is on the role of resilience models in explaining the behavioral trajectories of children in schools.

Russell Skiba is Professor in the School Psychology Program at Indiana University. He received his doctorate from the University of Minnesota. He most recently directed the Safe and Responsive Schools Project, funded by a U.S. Department of Education Projects of National Significance grant. He worked with eleven schools in two states to develop comprehensive and preventive approaches to ensuring school safety. He has presented on school violence prevention for associations and school districts throughout the country and recently received the Operation PUSH/Rainbow Coalition *Push for Excellence* award for his research in minority disproportionality in school suspension.

Dewey G. Cornell is a clinical psychologist and Professor of Education in the Curry School of Education at the University of Virginia. Dr. Cornell is Director of the UVA Youth Violence Project and is a faculty associate of the Institute of Law, Psychiatry, and Public Policy. He holds the Curry Memorial Chair in Education. One of his current projects concerns the development and implementation of guidelines for schools to use in responding to student threats of violence.

Issues in School Violence Research

CONTENTS

INTRODUCTION

Issues in School Violence Research

Edwin R. Gerler, Jr.

On December 16, 2002, I received an e-mail message from Michael Furlong, University of California, Santa Barbara, proposing a publication focused on *Issues in School Violence Research*. As I write the introduction for this publication, the 2003 December holiday season is upon us. In that space of time, Michael's idea has become a reality. With his colleagues Gale Morrison (also from the University of California, Santa Barbara), Russell Skiba (Indiana University), and Dewey Cornell (University of Virginia), Michael has brought together a collection of articles that address significant measurement and methodological issues in school violence research.

The lead article, "Methodological and Measurement Issues in School Violence Research: Moving Beyond the Social Problem Era," is the foundation piece for this publication. The article focuses on methodological pitfalls and critical measurement issues that hinder research progress in several related areas, including the uncertain reliability and

Edwin R. Gerler, Jr. is affiliated with North Carolina State University.

[Haworth co-indexing entry note]: "Issues in School Violence Research." Gerler, Jr., Edwin R. Co-published simultaneously in *Journal of School Violence* (The Haworth Press, Inc.) Vol. 3, No. 2/3, 2004, pp. 1-3; and: *Issues in School Violence Research* (ed: Michael J. Furlong et al.) The Haworth Press, Inc., 2004, pp. 1-3. Single or multiple copies of this article are available for a fee from The Haworth Document Delivery Service [1-800-HAWORTH, 9:00 a.m. - 5:00 p.m. (EST). E-mail address: docdelivery@haworthpress.com].

http://www.haworthpress.com/web/JSV
© 2004 by The Haworth Press, Inc. All rights reserved.
Digital Object Identifier: 10.1300/J202v03n02_01

validity of self-report surveys used to measure high-risk behavior and bullying, the limitations of discipline referral databases as a source of information on school climate, and the overly narrow focus on relatively infrequent critical incidents of violence, often at the expense of a more comprehensive and multifactorial examination of the school environment.

The other articles in this publication cover research challenges related to a variety of school violence areas.

"Warning Signs of Problems in Schools: Ecological Perspectives and Effective Practices for Combating School Aggression and Violence" provides information that helps educators assess their own schools and classrooms in an effort to promote a climate that will prevent violence and aggression.

"Using Office Referral Records in School Violence Research: Possibilities and Limitations" examines the sources of error that enter into the collection and use of office referrals. This article documents the importance of considering the ways office referral data provide information about how discipline systems are functioning on a school campus. The authors provide guidelines for utilizing disciplinary data for school safety and school policy planning.

"Identification of Bullies and Victims: A Comparison of Methods" examines the use of self-report data in studies of school violence. Bullying studies, for example, frequently rely on student self-report to identify bullies and victims of bullying, but research in the broader field of peer aggression makes greater use of other informants, especially peers, to identify aggressors and victims. This article raises concerns about reliance on student self-reports of bullying and bully victimization.

"Data Quality in Student Risk Behavior Surveys and Administrator Training" considers the importance of training school staff in survey administration and the value of examining survey instruments for validity in order to improve the accuracy of student self-report surveys.

"An Examination of the Reliability, Data Screening Procedures, and Extreme Response Patterns for the Youth Risk Behavior Surveillance Survey" explores psychometric characteristics of the Youth Risk Behavior Surveillance Survey (YRBS), one of the most widely used instruments to assess the prevalence of violent and other high-risk behaviors in secondary school settings. Overall, the results suggest an extreme response bias among some participants that may impact the validity of the YRBS instrument. More specifically, presence of this response bias may inflate estimates of the prevalence of school violence and related concerns. These findings are discussed in light of the need to carefully examine individual response patterns on future administrations of the YRBS in an effort to ensure maximum instrument utility.

"Structural Equation Modeling of School Violence Data: Methodological Considerations" examines methodological challenges associated with structural equation modeling (SEM) and structured means modeling (SMM) in research on school violence and related topics in the social and behavioral sciences.

"Beyond Guns, Drugs and Gangs: The Structure of Student Perceptions of School Safety" considers potential problems with school violence surveys. The article particularly examines the problems with construct validity that may result from the failure of researchers to consider key factors that contribute to violence.

I hope that the matters addressed here will stimulate new and better inquiry into the climate within which school violence occurs. In the lead article the editors summarize the purpose of this publication and offer an invitation to the research community:

> School violence and safety research will move forward and make unique scientific contributions only if it develops a core literature that critically examines its measurement, methods, and data analysis techniques. Such analysis becomes increasingly necessary as the field moves beyond its origins in affirming the presence of a social problem toward understanding the dynamics that uniquely contribute to the occurrence and suppression of aggression and violence, in all of its forms, on school campuses. This publication represents our first contribution to this endeavor. We welcome the research community's expansion on this effort.

ARTICLES

Methodological and Measurement Issues in School Violence Research: Moving Beyond the Social Problem Era

Michael J. Furlong
Gale M. Morrison
Dewey G. Cornell
Russell Skiba

Michael J. Furlong is Professor, University of California, Santa Barbara, Gevirtz Graduate School of Education, Santa Barbara, CA 93106 (E-mail: mfurlong@education.ucsb.edu). He is also affiliated with the Center for School-Based Youth Development.

Gale M. Morrison is Professor, University of California, Santa Barbara, Gevirtz Graduate School of Education, Santa Barbara, CA 93106 (E-mail: gale@education.ucsb.edu). She is also affiliated with the Center for School-Based Youth Development.

Dewey G. Cornell is Professor, Curry School of Education, University of Virginia, 405 Emmet Street, Charlottesville, VA 22903-2495 (E-mail: dcornell@virginia.edu). He is also Director of the Youth Violence Project.

Russell Skiba is Professor, Counseling and Educational Psychology, Indiana University, Center for Evaluation and Educaton Policy, 509 E. Third Street, Bloomington, IN 47401 (E-mail: skiba@indiana.edu).

Address correspondence to Michael J. Furlong.

[Haworth co-indexing entry note]: "Methodological and Measurement Issues in School Violence Research: Moving Beyond the Social Problem Era." Furlong, Michael J. et al. Co-published simultaneously in *Journal of School Violence* (The Haworth Press, Inc.) Vol. 3, No. 2/3, 2004, pp. 5-12; and: *Issues in School Violence Research* (ed: Michael J. Furlong et al.) The Haworth Press, Inc., 2004, pp. 5-12. Single or multiple copies of this article are available for a fee from The Haworth Document Delivery Service [1-800-HAWORTH, 9:00 a.m. - 5:00 p.m. (EST). E-mail address: docdelivery@haworthpress.com].

http://www.haworthpress.com/web/JSV
© 2004 by The Haworth Press, Inc. All rights reserved.
Digital Object Identifier: 10.1300/J202v03n02_02

SUMMARY. School violence became a topic of broad national concern in the United States in reaction to a series of tragic school shootings during the 1990s. Efforts to understand and prevent school shootings have stimulated the rapid development of a broader interest in school safety with an emerging multidisciplinary research agenda. The maturation and fulfillment of this research agenda require that researchers critically examine their research methods and measurement strategies. This article introduces a volume that examines fundamental methodological and measurement issues in the rapidly expanding body of research on school safety and violence. The authors hope to stimulate greater attention to methodological pitfalls and critical measurement issues that hinder research progress in several related areas, including the uncertain reliability and validity of self-report surveys used to measure high-risk behavior and bullying, the limitations of discipline referral databases as a source of information on school climate, and the overly narrow focus on relatively infrequent critical incidents of violence, often at the expense of a more comprehensive and multifactorial examination of the school environment. *[Article copies available for a fee from The Haworth Document Delivery Service: 1-800-HAWORTH. E-mail address: <docdelivery@haworthpress.com> Website: <http://www.HaworthPress.com> © 2004 by The Haworth Press, Inc. All rights reserved.]*

KEYWORDS. Measurement, school violence, methodological, school safety, school environment

School violence was a largely unacknowledged social problem prior to the 1990s (Furlong & Morrison, 2000). Between 1979 and 1992, there were 210 references in the *National Newspaper Index* under the keyword "school violence," but since 1993 there have been 1,291 reports focusing on school violence, clearly identifying school violence as an important social problem. The professional literature mirrors the mass media's pattern–currently there are only 21 publications prior to 1993 listed in the PsycINFO database under the school violence keyword but 296 publications during the past decade. From a historical perspective, school violence publications were driven more by public events (particularly school shootings) than by a well-considered research agenda. As a result, the rapidly developing professional literature often focused on the obvious need to prevent school violence, with little attention given to methodological and measurement issues (Furlong, Morrison, & Pavelski, 2000). It quickly became apparent, however, that knowledge about the nature and scope of school violence, as well as trends over time was incomplete, at best. Despite an inadequate knowledge base, the pressing concern with school violence as a social problem stimulated numerous calls to take action. In their meta-analysis of school violence prevention programs, Derzon and Wilson (1999) noted that there were two school violence review articles published for each empirical study of school violence, suggesting that empirically derived knowledge about school violence was not keeping pace with public interest and the demand for information to inform public policy.

The U.S. Federal government supported the development and widespread dissemination of three school violence prevention documents (Dwyer, Osher, & Warger, 1999; Osher & Dwyer, 2000; Osher, Dwyer, & Jackson, 2003). These documents contain highly plausible and thoughtful advice for school authorities based on a limited knowledge base but has not been accompanied by a systematic research effort to validate specific recommendations and practices.

The demand for immediate information about school violence precluded the possibility of careful development of new research measures. As a result, the first national report on school safety (U.S. Departments of Education and Justice, 1999) drew upon existing national studies such as the *Youth Risk Behavior Surveillance Survey* (e.g., Brener, Simon, Krug, & Lowry, 1999), the *National Crime Victimization Survey* (e.g., Hawkins, Herrenkohl, Farrington, Brewer, Catalano, Harachi, & Cothern, 2000), and the *Monitoring the Future Study* (e.g., Johnston, O'Malley, & Bachman [1996]). These well-regarded, periodic surveys were adapted to bootstrap information about student experiences with violence on school campuses. Such efforts might be regarded as a hallmark of the social problem era of research on school violence.

Perhaps the most significant effort to assess school violence came through adaptations of the CDC's *Youth Risk Behavior Survey* (Kann et al., 1996). The Center for Disease Control (CDC) incorporated violence items into their ongoing surveillance surveys. CDC findings were reported in the first National Safe School Report before any peer-reviewed research article about the reliability and validity of the YRBS school safety items was published. Moreover, the early results from YRBS surveys were widely publicized without qualification or careful explanation. For example, CDC announced in early YRBS surveys that more than 1 in 5 "high school students" carried a weapon each month. Of course, the early YRBS questions did not specify school as the location of the weapon possession. News media statements such as "20% in high schools found to carry weapons" (*The New York Times*, 1991, October 11) could easily be misinterpreted to mean that students were carrying weapons to school. Furthermore, survey questions about weapon carrying did not discriminate possession of a weapon for activities such as hunting or camping from weapon possession that was intended for interpersonal violence.

VOLUME ORGANIZATION AND OVERVIEW

With the publication of the *Journal of School Violence* it can be argued that "school violence" as a topic of scientific inquiry has matured into a recognized field of study. We contend that research on school violence is ready to move beyond the social problem era when researchers responded to immediate needs for information and lacked time and opportunity to consider methodological and measurement issues. We believe that it is timely to examine the methodological challenges that are associated with this new, multidisciplinary field of study and to begin to articulate standards for the scientific credibility of its research methods and findings. The purpose of this volume is to advance that process.

Osher, VanAcker, Morrison, Gable, Dwyer, and Quinn (2004) provide a discussion of school-level warning signs for school aggression and violence. These authors present this information as a complement and extension to the well-known documents *Early Warning, Timely Response: A Guide to Safe Schools* (Dwyer, Osher, & Warger, 1998) and *Safeguarding Our Children: An Action Guide* (Dwyer & Osher, 2003). While the 1998 *Warning Signs* document focused on individual student warning signs, the article in this issue is intended to focus attention and future measurement work on school-level contributions to aggressive and violent student behavior. In doing so, the authors present an analysis of school, classroom, family, and individual contexts for aggressive behavior and suggest tools for assessing these important ecological indicators.

Morrison, Peterson, O'Farrell, and Redding (2004) explore the utility school discipline data, perhaps the most "naturally occurring" data on school misbehavior and aggression. They note that there is very little information available in professional or research literature about the reliability and validity of these data. Their article provides an examination of the sources of error that enter into the collection and use of these data and focuses particularly on office referral data, as these data constitute the most common information available on school campuses. The authors highlight monitoring misbehavior as one purpose of counting and categorizing office referrals but note that another important purpose of office referrals for school safety is to analyze and characterize the school discipline process and resulting climate and context for student behavior. They provide guidelines for how best to utilize information about behavior and discipline systems for school safety research.

Cornell and Brockenbrough (2004) examine measurement issues related to bullying, perhaps the most pervasive and widely recognized form of violence that occurs in schools. Their results show that there is only modest correspondence among three methods for identifying bullies and victims of bullying, and that peers identify far more students as bullies and bully victims than do either teacher nomination or self-report methods. Furthermore, identification as a bully by peers and teachers, but not self-identification, was predictive of school discipline referrals, detentions, and suspensions over the subsequent six months. Their results raise questions about the widespread reliance on student self-reports of bullying, and point to the need for careful validation of existing methods for identifying bullies and victims of bullying.

Cross and Newman-Gonchar (2004) utilize data gathered as part of one site's implementation of the Safe School/Healthy Student Initiative (Furlong, Osher, & Paige, 2003). They examine standard validity checks across three different school violence and safety surveys and found that fewer students gave contradictory responses to surveys given routinely or in conjunction with a specific educational unit (treatment groups) than they did to surveys administered on short notice or not in conjunction with any instructional units (control groups). In addition to effects related to who administered the surveys, it was found that incidence rates were influenced when inconsistent and extreme responses were controlled.

Furlong, Sharkey, Bates, and Smith (2004) use the 2001 YRBS database to examine the presence and influence of cases in which students give the most extreme response options for school violence, safety and risk-related items. They provide an overview of issues related to the reliability of the YRBS and further explore the response patterns of a subset of 414 youths who gave the most extreme response (6 or more times in the past month) to the item that asked about the frequency of school weapon possession, They found that this group of extreme weapon-item responders were more likely to also give extreme responses to other school risk behavior items as well as positive health behavior items.

Their findings suggest that a subset of the YRBS cases may reflect a type of extreme response pattern that is uncontrolled for in virtually all research using the YRBS.

In addition to exploring the reliability of core school violence and safety instrument, Mayer (2004) examines challenges and limitations faced when using structural equation modeling (SEM) and structured means modeling (SMM) to analyze processes associated with school violence and disruption. As researchers increasingly examine more complex, multilevel model of school violence and disruption, the appropriate use of complex statistical modeling techniques will be an increasing concern.

Finally, Skiba, Simmons, Peterson, McKelvey, Forde, and Gallini (2004) note that extant national surveys are based on an understanding of school violence that is driven primarily by critical incidents or criminal violations. Yet most current theoretical models of school violence and its prevention emphasize a comprehensive perspective that encompasses both serious incidents *and* day-to-day disruption and climate issues. Further, very few reports on existing school safety surveys use empirical procedures, such as factor analysis, to derive their dimensions or subscales. Skiba et al. report on the development and technical characteristics of a comprehensive self-report survey for secondary students, the *Safe and Responsive Schools Safe Schools Survey.* Survey items were drawn from both school safety and school climate surveys in order to represent a more comprehensive model of school violence. Their results suggest that both major safety items and day-to-day discipline/climate issues shape student perceptions of school safety. Indeed, regression analyses suggest that student perceptions of climate may in some cases be a better predictor of perceptions of overall school safety than serious violence.

CONCLUSION

This volume is possible only because many researchers and educators have recognized the need to better understand school violence as a social problem. Their openness and sensitivity focused attention on this issue, and their interest began the development of knowledge about its occurrence. The various national studies, task forces, and research efforts to date have provided core information and moved the field of school violence research forward in essential ways.

At this time, however, the results presented in this volume present a challenge to the school violence research community. School violence and safety research will move forward and make unique scientific contributions only if it develops a core literature that critically examines its measurement, methods, and data analysis techniques. Such analysis becomes increasingly necessary as the field moves beyond its origins in affirming the presence of a social problem toward understanding the dynamics that uniquely contribute to the occurrence and suppression of aggression and violence, in all of its forms, on school campuses. This publication represents our first contribution to this endeavor. We welcome the research community's expansion on this effort.

REFERENCES

Brener, N. D., Simon, T. R., Krug, E. G., & Lowry, R. (1999). Recent trends in violence-related behaviors among high school students in the United States. *Journal of the American Medical Association, 282,* 440-446.

Cornell, D. G., & Brockenbrough, K. (2004). Identification of bullies and victims: A comparison of methods. *Journal of School Violence, 3*(2/3), 63-87.

Cross, J. E., & Newman-Gonchar, R. (2004). Data quality in student risk behavior surveys and administrator training. *Journal of School Violence, 3*(2/3), 89-108.

Derzon, J. H., & Wilson, S. J. (1999). *An empirical review of school-based programs to reduce violence.* Washington, DC: Hamilton Fish Institute, George Washington University. Retrieved August 25, 2003, from http://hamfish.org/resources/record/6/

Dwyer, K., & Osher, D. (2000). *Safeguarding our children: An action guide.* Washington, DC: U.S. Departments of Education and Justice, American Institutes of Research. Retrieved December 15, 2002, from http://cecp.air.org/guide/actionguide.htm

Dwyer, K., Osher, D., & Warger, C. (1998). *Early warning, timely response: A guide to safe schools.* Washington, DC: U.S. Department of Education. Retrieved December 15, 2002, from www.air-dc.org/cecp/guide/annotated.htm

Furlong, M. J., & Morrison, G. M. (2000). The school in school violence: Definitions and facts. *Journal of Emotional & Behavioral Disorders, 8,* 71-82.

Furlong, M. J., Morrison, G. M. & Pavelski, R. (2000). Trends in school psychology for the 21st century: Influences of school violence on professional change. *Psychology in the Schools* (Special Issue: School psychology and the 21st century: Millennium issue), *37,* 81-90.

Furlong, M. J., Osher, D., & Paige, L. (2003). The Safe Schools/Healthy Students (SS/HS) initiative: Lessons learned from implementing comprehensive youth development programs. *Psychology in the Schools, 40,* 447-456.

Furlong, M. J., Sharkey, J. D., Bates, M. P., & Smith, D. C. (2004). An examination of the reliability, data screening procedures, and extreme response patterns for the Youth Risk Behavior Surveillance Survey. *Journal of School Violence, 3*(2/3), 109-130.

Hawkins, J. D., Herrenkohl, T. I., Farrington, D. P., Brewer, D., Catalano, R. F., Harachi, T. W., & Cothern, L. (2000). *Predictors of youth violence.* U.S. Department of Justice: Office of Juvenile Justice and Delinquency Prevention.

Johnston, L. D., O'Malley, P. M., & Bachman, J. G. (1996). *National survey results on drug use from Monitoring the Future Study, 1975-1995: Volume I Secondary School Students.* Washington, DC: U.S. Government Printing Office (NIH Publication No. 96-4139).

Kann, L., Warren, C. W., Harris, W. A., Collins, J. L., Douglas, K. A., Williams, B. I. et al. (1996). Youth risk behavior surveillance-United States, 1995. *Journal of School Health, 66,* 365-377.

Mayer, M. J. (2004). Structural equation modeling of school violence data: Methodological considerations. *Journal of School Violence, 3*(2/3), 131-148.

Morrison, G. M., Peterson, R., O'Farrell, S., & Redding, M. (2004). Using office referral records in school violence research: Possibilities and limitations. *Journal of School Violence, 3*(2/3), 39-61.

The New York Times. (1991, October 11). 20% in high schools found to carry weapons. *141,* pA13(L).

Osher, D., Dwyer, K., & Jackson, S. (2003). *Safe, supportive, and successful schools: Step by step.* Longmont, CO: Sopris West.

Osher, D., VanAcker, R., Morrison, G. M., Gable, R., Dwyer, K., & Quinn, M. (2004). Warning signs of problems in schools: Ecological perspectives and effective practices for combating school aggression and violence. *Journal of School Violence, 3*(2/3), 13-37.

Skiba, R., Simmons, A. B., Peterson, R., McKelvey, J., Forde, S., & Gallini, S. (2004). Beyond guns, drugs and gangs: The structure of student perceptions of school safety. *Journal of School Violence, 3*(2/3), 149-171.

U.S. Departments of Education and Justice. (1999). *1999 annual report on school safety.* Retrieved August 1, 2003, from http://www.safetyzone.org/pdf/schoolsafety2.pdf

Warning Signs of Problems in Schools: Ecological Perspectives and Effective Practices for Combating School Aggression and Violence

David Osher
Richard VanAcker
Gale M. Morrison
Robert Gable
Kevin Dwyer
Mary Quinn

SUMMARY. One need not look hard to find evidence of concern related to the nature of student behavior in our schools. School violence,

David Osher is Managing Research Scientist, American Institutes for Research, 10720 Columbia Pike, Suite 500, Silver Spring, MD 20901.

Richard VanAcker is Associate Professor of Education, University of Illinois at Chicago, 3444 EPASW, College of Education, 1040 West Harrison M/C 147, Chicago, IL 60607.

Gale M. Morrison is Professor, Gevirtz Graduate School of Education, University of California, Santa Barbara, Santa Barbara, CA 93106.

Robert Gable is Eminent Scholar, Old Dominion University, Child Study Center, Norfolk, VA 23529.

Kevin Dwyer is Senior Education Advisor, American Institutes for Research, 10720 Columbia Pike, Suite 500, Silver Spring, MD 20901.

Mary Quinn is Principal Research Scientist, American Institutes for Research, 10720 Columbia Pike, Suite 500, Silver Spring, MD 20901.

Address correspondence to David Osher via e-mail at <dosher@air.org>.

[Haworth co-indexing entry note]: "Warning Signs of Problems in Schools: Ecological Perspectives and Effective Practices for Combating School Aggression and Violence." Osher, David et al. Co-published simultaneously in *Journal of School Violence* (The Haworth Press, Inc.) Vol. 3, No. 2/3, 2004, pp. 13-37; and: *Issues in School Violence Research* (ed: Michael J. Furlong et al.) The Haworth Press, Inc., 2004, pp. 13-37. Single or multiple copies of this article are available for a fee from The Haworth Document Delivery Service [1-800-HAWORTH, 9:00 a.m. - 5:00 p.m. (EST). E-mail address: docdelivery@haworthpress.com].

http://www.haworthpress.com/web/JSV
© 2004 by The Haworth Press, Inc. All rights reserved.
Digital Object Identifier: 10.1300/J202v03n02_03

aggression, bullying, and harassment (e.g., racial or sexual) are often cited as challenging behaviors confronting educators and community leaders. Unfortunately, most schools address these concerns with aversive consequences delivered to individual perpetrators in a hope of reducing the future probability of undesired behavior. A growing body of literature identifies the need to explore the social context of behavior. The community, school, classroom, family, and peer group interact with student characteristics to help prevent, support the development of, and even exacerbate the display of both desired and undesired behavior. This article applies the logic of warning signs and functional behavioral assessment to schools as it explores the social context of the school and the classroom. The school-wide and classroom-based factors that have been associated with or found to support problem behaviors are discussed. Information is provided that will allow educators to assess their own schools and classrooms in an effort to promote a climate that will aid in the prevention of violence and aggression. *[Article copies available for a fee from The Haworth Document Delivery Service: 1-800-HAWORTH. E-mail address: <docdelivery@haworthpress.com> Website: <http://www.HaworthPress. com> © 2004 by The Haworth Press, Inc. All rights reserved.]*

KEYWORDS. Aggression, school violence, bullying, harassment, social context

In June 1998, in response to the wave of rage shootings in U.S. high schools, President Clinton asked the Secretary of Education and the Attorney General to convene an expert panel to identify the early warning signs of school violence. The expert panelists stated that there was little point in identifying early warning signs if the guide did not also address the school environment (Dwyer, Osher, & Hoffman, 2000). This ecological framework was incorporated in the publications that flowed from that work: *Early Warning, Timely Response: A Guide to Safe Schools* (Dwyer, Osher, & Warger, 1998) and *Safeguarding Our Children: An Action Guide* (Dwyer & Osher, 2000). The framework has also been incorporated in other discussions of violence prevention and in policy documents (e.g., Elliott, Grady, Shaw, Aultman-Bettridge, & Beaulieu, 2000) and is consistent with meta-analyses of prevention interventions (e.g., Catalano, Berglund, Ryan, Lonczak, & Hawkins, 2002; Wilson, Gottfredson, & Najaka, 2001).

Terminology such as "early warning signs" has metaphorical as well as instrumental functions. These metaphors affect how individuals approach problems (Hobbs, 1982; Osher, 1996). Ecological frameworks, which emphasize the importance of social environments (e.g., Brofenbrenner, 1977; Felner, 2000), are not intuitive to many Americans. We live in an individualistic culture and are attracted by intrapsychic and individualized explanations of social phenomena (Bellah et al., 1985; Ryan, 1972). For example, resilience is often treated as an individual phenomenon, ignoring the role of social support (Osher, Kendziora, VanDenBerg, & Dennis, 1999). Similarly, discussions of early warning signs usually focus on individual risk factors rather than on environmental risk factors. Ecological explanations have not had a powerful impact on the mental maps of educators and policy makers. This limits the appeal of the multifaceted interventions required to prevent youth violence (e.g., Tolan & Guerra, 1994).

This article is intended to be conceptual and heuristic, helping us think about alternative ways of using early warning signs. It has three objectives: (a) extend the ongoing discussion regarding the relationship between school ecology and school violence, (b) spur research in this area, and (c) facilitate the development and use of tools designed to identify variables related to the school and classroom contexts that impact on student behavior. In the following discussion, we analyze the school context of aggression and violence, examine school warning signs at the campus-wide and classroom levels, identify tools that can be employed to assess schools, and identify research needs. We conclude by applying the logic of functional assessment to examine why schools implement practices that interfere with the promotion of student success.

SCHOOL CONTEXT OF AGGRESSION AND VIOLENCE

The social context of the school affects behavioral (as well as academic) outcomes (Reynolds & Teddlie, 2000). The organizational structure and culture, human technical and financial resources, tone, physical plant, and social capital of schools all affect faculty behavior and student outcomes (Fullan & Hargreaves, 1996; Smey-Richman, 1991), both through their direct impact on students and faculty and as mediated by their effects on students and faculty. The organizational structure of the school mediates human relationships. For example, it is harder to build community in large schools, but these schools can be broken down into smaller academies where it is easier for teachers to know the students and their families (e.g., Mc Andrews & Anderson, 2002).

Changing structures may facilitate change, but it does not ensure it (Fullan & Hargreaves, 1996). Culture also plays a key role. For example, Rosenholtz (1989) distinguished the cultural characteristics of learning impovished ("stuck") and learning enriched ("moving") schools. Culture includes the norms and beliefs (e.g., about teaching), values (e.g., about competition), rituals (e.g., honors ceremonies), and shared sense of efficacy (e.g., "we can teach these students"). Culture also includes expectations regarding the roles that members of the school community play (e.g., does teaching include student support) and how people interact (e.g., teaching occurs in isolation). Culture can be explicit (e.g., a mission statement) or taken for granted (e.g., all materials are in English).

Structure and culture are interactive (Lortie, 1975). While the structure of the school provides role expectations for teachers, culture fleshes out and reinforces the nature of the role. They come together in what some describe as the school environment, which also includes the ambiance (the palpable feel or tone) of the school (Nias, Southworth, & Yeomans, 1989).

School context involves resources: staff capacity, physical plant, technologies, finances, and social capital. Staff capacity includes the skills and experiences of individual members: leadership technical, affective, and interpersonal skills. The physical plant structures interactions (e.g., the size of hallways) as well as perceptions of safety. Technologies include knowledge-based tools (e.g., functional assessment) and physical tools (e.g., assistive technology). Financial resources involve both funding and the efficiency with which funds are used (Osher, Quinn, Rutherford, & Poirier, 2003). Social capital includes both the relational trust of students, faculty, and staff (Bryk & Schneider, 2002) and the ability to draw on local and national community for human and financial resources. Schools can build these resources. For example, schools can build (or sustain) the capacity of teachers to care through an infrastructure of support, which includes adequate staffing, staff development, and consultation (Quinn, Osher, Hoffman, & Hanley, 1998).

Every student is unique, having different temperaments, coping skills, and styles of responding. Individual differences in and among students require support and attention from skilled adults to maximize learning academic and social emotional skills. Accommodations can significantly reduce barriers to learning, and strength-based individualized instruction and mental health promotion can enhance success and motivation. A poorly developed curriculum unaligned with past instruction may exacerbate minor learning problems for some children. A failure to attend to the social and emotional development of students can undermine their ability to regulate their behavior and to interact with one another (Greenberg et al., 2003). A poorly organized school can overwhelm some students, make it hard to teach, or set the stage for violence (Dwyer & Osher, 2000; Osher, Sandler, & Nelson, 2001).

SCHOOL-LEVEL WARNING SIGNS

A school–as a unit, as a conglomerate, as a systemic whole–has an impact on school safety. Specific aspects of a school can put students at risk above and beyond other risk factors (Furlong & Morrison, 2000). For example, Gottfredson and Gottfredson (1985) analyzed safe school data from more than 600 schools and found that school characteristics as well as community characteristics contributed to teacher and student victimization rates. Factors that they identified included a lack of teaching resources, large school size (junior high schools), and larger number of different students taught during the day (high schools). Similarly, Mayer and colleagues (e.g., Mayer, Butterworth, Nafpaktitis, & Sulzer-Azaroff, 1983) demonstrated that ambiguous sanctions, punitive teacher attitudes, and poor cooperation between high school teachers and administrators could increase the rates of problem behavior and alienate students. Ostroff (1992) found that teacher satisfaction and commitment predicted student disciplinary problems. Finally, Bryk and Driscoll (1988) and Bryk, Lee, and Holland (1993) found that communal organization decreased behavior problems, whereas large school size increased them. Table 1 provides some indicators of a troubled school.

The School Environment. The physical climate is a strong indicator for safe or unsafe schools. Physical indicators of an unsafe school include an unattractive or unclean physical plant, the presence of graffiti or extensive damage, the dominant display of fences or metal detectors, and crowded halls and public spaces coupled with lack of adult supervision. Although screening for weapons may be a necessary practice for some schools, the humanity with which this screening takes place makes a statement about how students are welcomed to school. For example, Snyder, Morrison, and Smith (1996) describe a method of screening students for weapons used by an assistant principal in an urban school. On entering the school building, each student is greeted by a smile and a welcoming greeting while being checked for weapons. This

TABLE 1. Indicators of a Troubled School

Environment

- Damage or vandalism to the school building is obvious; the building is in general disrepair or a state of neglect
- Halls are crowded and chaotic during transitions
- Notices for student activities are not evident
- School grounds are littered and unclean; graffiti is present
- Notices about awards, special events, and special achievements are not displayed
- School symbols, mascots, and colors are not evident

Student Behavior

- Students themselves may appear less than friendly
- Students push and shove one another
- Put-downs and teasing between students are common
- Strong social cliques are present
- Students are wandering around in halls during class time
- Students and faculty leave campus as soon as school is over
- Evidence of extramural student participation is not evident

Faculty/Staff Behavior

- Students may be scolded in public; what teachers generally notice are things students are doing wrong
- Adults in cafeteria bunch together at one table, talking and ignoring bullying
- Visitors are not greeted or welcomed; no one greets you as you enter the office–you are ignored
- Counselors are too busy administering meetings to be available to students
- Teachers say that they do not know how to get help for behavior problems and do not think that their pleas for help will be heard
- Adult supervision is not visible
- Staff treat students disrespectfully
- No teachers greet or interact with students in a friendly and welcoming manner
- Staff are not attentive to visitors or students when they enter the office
- Support services personnel are rarely on campus
- Staff talk negatively about students, families, and the community
- Staff talk about their inability to make a difference
- Staff and administrators talk negatively about each other
- Teachers do not feel a responsibility for outcomes and blame students for failure
- Teachers have no conceptual framework with which to establish an instructional management system aligned with group and individual needs of students
- Level/token systems lack the capacity to individualize
- Teaching of English vocabulary is not culturally connected; words are taught with white, middle-class images
- Excessive disciplinary referrals occur

School Policy

- No active PTA is present
- An excessive number of rules are present and are expressed negatively
- Counterproductive policies exclude students (e.g., locking out tardy students)
- Informal in-school suspensions are used to keep behavior issues off the books
- Problem-solving meetings are held without preparation–not even the student's records are available
- Monolingual parents are notified in writing in English only
- Many students sit in the office after being kicked out of class
- A stranger goes unnoticed on campus
- No one observes teaching
- An excessive emphasis is placed on competition

approach maintains the physical safety of school participants while setting a tone of welcome and caring for students.

The educational climate also has an impact on the extent to which students and staff feel safe and productive. Behavioral and academic goals and processes of a school go hand in hand. Effective schools have high positive academic expectations, supported by effective instructional strategies, a focus on skill acquisition, appropriate monitoring of student progress, and parent and community involvement (Reynolds, Teddlie, Creemers, Scheerens, & Townsend, 2000). An absence of these expectations and supports for academic achievement is a warning sign.

The extent to which the indicators above are achieved depends on the quality of the school leadership and the relationships that are fostered between leaders and staff, between staff members, between staff and students, and between students. Our experience suggests that signs of unsafe and ineffective schools include lack of agreement among staff about school policies and practices for learning and behavior; lack of training and support for implementing policies and practices; poor staff morale; disrespectful treatment of students; and disrespect between students characterized by bullying, isolation, fighting, and teasing.

At the policy level, discipline practices affect the extent to which the school is orderly and efficient as opposed to disorganized and chaotic. Sugai and Horner (1999) outlined the components of effective schoolwide discipline practices: a clear statement of rules and expectations, consistently communicated and applied consequences for rule-breaking behavior, concrete efforts to teach students appropriate behavior, and positive consequences for positive behavior. The warning signs for a school environment that threatens the safety of its students can be characterized as unclear expectations, inconsistent and punitive application of consequences, and few opportunities for students to learn positive behaviors.

Another warning sign is an absence of systematic data collection. Effective schools systematically analyze available data to assess their progress on major goals and objectives. Similarly, the use of continual data analysis to examine disciplinary office referrals (number, type of offense, who refers, who offends) has been identified as a critical feature of successful positive behavior support programs (Sugai, Sprague, Horner, & Walker, 2000). Other broader indicators of school ineffectiveness are high rates of absenteeism, retention, dropout, and school mobility. Although students may change schools as parents seek to avoid ineffective schools, some students also experience nonnormative mobility–they move between classes and schools for school-discipline-driven reasons (Osher, Morrison, & Bailey, 2003).

Finally, the absence of resources can be a warning sign. Resources include personnel, training opportunities, procedures, and programs. Pupil personnel staff, such as school counselors or school psychologists to assist with the noninstructional, social, and emotional needs of children can help teachers who struggle to instruct students who experience multiple challenges in their lives. Programs and processes that create a schoolwide foundation and provide for early and intensive intervention are also important (Dwyer & Osher, 2000).

Warning Signs Related to School-Family Relationships. Families play a key role in supporting positive school outcomes (Henderson & Mapp, 2002). Although we know a good deal about how to foster family-school collaboration, a "disconnect" frequently exists between families and schools, particularly when differences of race, ethnicity, language, and class are present (Epstein, 1995; Osher, 2000). Families may distrust school staff, and school staff may perceive parents as being problems (Bryk & Schnieder, 2002).

Poor family-school relations have multiple warning signs. Some are behavioral, such as the types of contact that parents have with schools and the causes and level of their participation. Schools with similar demographic characteristics vary in the percentage of parents participating in parent-teacher meetings, special education planning, and public assemblies. Similarly the predominant reason for parent participation may be family driven or school driven (e.g., a summons to address a child's behavior). Limited parent-driven participation is a warning sign.

Others indicators are attitudinal and cultural. Schools vary in how welcome they make parents feel. Parents may experience suspicion, disrespect, or apathy. Similarly parents may hear from the school only when their child is not doing well or feel blamed for their child's behavior or devalued because of their economic status or culture. Similarly, staff may have low expectations of families, see families as obstacles rather than resources, or define family involvement and support in ethnocentric terms that do not recognize the different definitions of family as well as the different ways families support their children (e.g., Hulsebosch & Logan, 1998).

CLASSROOM-LEVEL WARNING SIGNS

In the classroom setting, a student must compete for attention from both the adults and the other children. Classroom norms and expectations may differ significantly from those of the child's family and cultural group. In the classroom, a student is called on to perform, often publicly, a variety of tasks and activities. Success or failure, too, is frequently indicated publicly. Thus, the classroom is a critical setting for enhancing student success or, conversely, exacerbating failure. Table 2 lists some indicators of a troubled classroom.

The physical setting of the classroom can provide important information about the nature of likely transactions. The physical space is a setting event that can bring about various behaviors (Conroy & Fox, 1994; Fox, 1990; Repp, 1994). The location, size, shape, and general state of repair of a classroom often indicate the value placed on the students and contribute to the nature of the activities that transpire (Fox & Conroy,

TABLE 2. Indicators of a Troubled Classroom

Environment

- Lack of care in making the physical appearance of the room attractive
- No student work displayed
- Lack of engaging materials
- Lack of organization and the room is often cluttered
- Excessive list of rules expressed negatively
- No evidence of positive behavioral goals–posted positive class rules
- No evidence of children's creativity–art, creative writing, cultural creations

Student Behavior

- Many students are not attending
- Students not working productively
- Students displaying disruptive behaviors
- Many students working in isolated parts of room
- Students are bored
- Students do not appear to understand the routine or there is no routine
- Students do passive seat work

Teacher Behavior

- Teacher sits behind desk while children are doing individual seat work although some are confused
- Teacher yelling or sarcasm
- Teacher does not know the IEP goals of students
- Teacher verbalizes frustration
- Teachers has no conceptual framework to direct instruction or classroom management
- Teacher resorts to punitive response for lack of involvement prior to trying to engage the student positively
- Lessons clearly do not "trap" all students and teacher makes little effort to interest student in the task
- Lesson planning does not appear obvious
- Instructional time is a small proportion when compared to time on behavioral control
- Instruction is not consistent with curriculum
- Little or no individualized instruction–students in classical three groups of learners
- No evidence of cooperative learning

1995; Sasso, Peck, & Garrison-Harrell, 1998). For example, one of the authors was asked to consult on the behavior of students in a class of students with behavioral disorders. The class was held in what was once the equipment storage room for the gymnasium. The room, which had no windows or other source of adequate ventilation, housed a teacher, an instructional aide, and nine students. For the observer to enter the classroom, two students had to leave their desks to allow passage to an open seat. The gym was still in use throughout the instructional day, and the sound of students engaging in physical education activities could be heard. Obviously, the physical setting had an impact on the students' behavior in this classroom. The room was cramped, stiflingly hot, and clearly not conducive to academic instruction. The nature of the setting provided numerous conditions that contributed to high rates of situational violence (e.g., as students violated each other's physical space out of necessity).

Other variables related to the physical setting have been found to contribute to student and teacher performance: the arrangement of the space, the room's cleanliness and organization, and the ability of the classroom to accommodate student needs, such as space to accommodate student mobility and the storage of personal belongings (McAfee, 1987; Ratcliff, 2001; Slavin, 1989). A number of questions are relevant to investigating the physical context of the classroom and its impact on behavior. Does the classroom's physical setting welcome the students? Does it indicate that this space belongs to them (e.g., the display of student-made materials or items of interest to the students)? Is there space for student belongings that might help support student ownership of the space? Does the setting facilitate the desired activities for a given lesson (e.g., student discussion, hands-on interaction)? Does the classroom provide a level of physical flexibility to accommodate the variety of activities taking place?

Even more important than the physical climate of the classroom is its emotional climate. Classrooms characterized by low rates of academic engagement, praise, and reinforcement and high rates of reprimand may actually encourage the behavior patterns of coercion and dominance (Farmer, Farmer, & Gut, 1999). The nature of the social exchanges among members of the classroom can be very informative about the general emotional climate. The frequency of pleasant social exchanges, the nature of the message, voice tone and intensity, and level of eye contact can communicate a significant amount of information related to the emotional climate of the classroom (National Institute of Child Health and Human Development, 2002). Are the actions of the adults and students in the classroom welcoming and accepting? Does the nature of the exchanges between members of the classroom support a sense of mutual caring and respect? Are students allowed to participate frequently and with enough success (e.g., level of correct responding) to promote their comfort and willingness to take social and academic risks? Are the expectations for student behavior clear and obvious from the point of entry through the course of the day? Do both the staff and the students understand these expectations? The subjective nature of these variables often makes it difficult to develop clear and objective operational definitions for data collection (Bakeman & Gottman, 1997). Their importance to the overall sense of student and teacher welfare, however, suggests that investigating these variables is critical for identifying the contextual factors that mark settings that promote student success (e.g., Levering, 2000).

The overall objective of the classroom is to provide a setting that promotes the social and academic development of the students. Obviously, information related to the effective delivery of the curriculum and instruction helps identify successful schools. The educational literature stresses the importance of establishing high expectations for student performance (e.g., Porter & Brophy, 1988). However, an effective teacher must be prepared to adapt the level of difficulty of the academic task on the basis of the specific abilities of the student being challenged. Does the teacher demonstrate knowledge of the diversity (e.g., academic, cultural, or linguistic) represented in the classroom? Does the teacher make the necessary accommodations to address student diversity? Are the lessons designed to incorporate and benefit from the students' diversity? Considerable research exists to guide educators on the development and delivery of effective lessons (e.g., Office of Educational Research, 1987). Nevertheless, far too often, classroom instruction is characterized by ineffective teaching (Beaman & Wheldall, 2000; Porter & Brophy, 1988). Data on the amount of time students actively engage in academics, the number of opportunities each student is given to respond, the frequency and nature of instructional interruptions and disturbances (e.g., stopping instruction to address behavioral infractions), and the level of correct responding can provide important insights into lesson delivery and student involvement. If the level of correct responding is too low, students may become disillusioned. Fear of failure and lack of success may result in a lack of persistence in the face of failure, learned helplessness, and a reduced sense of self-efficacy (Harter, 1999). Instructional probes and curriculum-based measures can help determine whether the nature of the instruction results in the desired instructional outcomes (Crawford, Tindal, & Stieber, 2001; Dunn & Eckert, 2002).

The interaction of teachers and students is particularly important in facilitating learning, supporting desired behavior, and connecting the child to the school. The planned and structured involvement of students in activities to promote the development of desired social and emotional skills must be considered (Sugai & Lewis, 1996; Wagner & Rutherford, 1996). Are students provided direct instruction related to social skills and social problem solving and is this instruction consistent with what we know about effective approaches (Greenberg et al., 2003)? If so, do adults model appropriate skills and do students have opportunities to incorporate them in their regular interactions? Are behavioral infractions addressed in ways that take advantage of effective teaching practices to promote desired alternative behavior? Are instructional or pedagogical consequences employed in response to undesired behavior (VanAcker, 2002)? Do planned and structured activities allow students to practice desired alternative behaviors with adequate feedback to support the adoption of these alternative behaviors?

The nature and conditional probability of feedback provided to students represent critical sources of data for identifying classroom environments that are either beneficial or detrimental to students. Unfortunately, considerable data suggest that teachers are generally much more likely to deliver reprimands for undesired student behavior (both academic and social) than they are to praise desired behavior (Beaman & Wheldall, 2000; Sutherland & Wehby, 2001a). This is especially true for students who are at an elevated risk for school failure. For example, Sutherland and Wehby (2001a) report that students with emotional and behavioral disorders are far less likely than typical students to be given opportunities to respond in class. Moreover, these same students receive far less praise and considerably more reprimands. Both the overall frequency of praise or reprimand and the ratio of praise to reprimands appear to be important. If the ratio of reprimand to praise favors reprimand, students may become increasingly disenfranchised with school and their pursuit of academic excellence (Sutherland, 2000).

If the teacher, overwhelmed by a large class, uses a stern or loud voice when calling a child's name, that child is likely to internalize the communication as rejection, criticism, failure, and punishment. The child may feel shame at not having the skill to perform the appropriate behavior or, sadly, may not even know the response the teacher expects. This confused child may be beginning a downward spiral toward hating school and progressively misbehaving or withdrawing socially. Similarly, a child whose language-processing skills are poor may not understand the directions and act out to avoid embarrassment. That child may even support the teacher's assumption of deliberate defiance to save face.

The conditional probability of a given consequence for behavior should also be examined. For example, VanAcker, Grant, and Henry (1996) found that in the same general education classrooms, students with an increased risk for displaying aggressive behavior experienced significantly different contingencies for their behavior. Praise for desired social behavior and for correct academic responding, although predictable over chance levels for students with medium to low levels of risk for aggression, was a random event, unrelated to the desired behavior of the most at-risk students. In too many classrooms, students are being given the message that "school is not for you" by the nature of the consequences provided.

The peer group within the classroom provides yet another important social context because peers exert considerable influence on one another's behavior (Coie, Dodge, & Kupersmidt, 1990). Peers provide or withhold attention and affiliation. Students seek information from their peers as a way to estimate their social competence, popularity, and ability in a variety of areas. Peer social networks that serve to establish, modify, and support the beliefs, attitudes, and behaviors of their members exist in classrooms (Farmer, VanAcker, Pearl, & Rodkin, 1999). Classroom social networks are not randomly formed. Rather, they appear to reflect both selection (self and environmental) and socialization processes that are influenced by a complex array of factors that includes, but extends beyond, students' social skills. Specifically, students differentially select, sort, and shape themselves into social networks of peer clusters that tend to comprise students who are similar to one another on salient social characteristics. Recent research has found that peer social networks can influence the display of both desired and undesired behavior (Rodkin, Farmer, Pearl, & VanAcker, 2000; Xie, Cairns, & Cairns, 1999). Social Cognitive Mapping (Cairns, Cairns, Neckerman, Gest, & Gariepy, 1988) can be used in classrooms to identify peer social networks and the key attributes of these various social groupings. This process employs students' reports of classroom peer clusters paired with teacher, self, and peer reports of behaviors to identify and classify peer social networks. This information can be used to discourage the formation of networks that foster undesired behavior and foster the development of and student involvement with prosocial networks.

TOOLS AND ASSESSMENT OF THE SCHOOL CONTEXT

An extensive literature identifies the relationship of school and classroom context variables and their impact on student behavior (e.g., Brophy, 1988). As a result, efforts to improve student academic achievement and social competence and to curb violence, aggression, and other challenging student behaviors require educators to become aware of the risk factors and problems that exist in their school setting. A wide variety of measures and assessment procedures are available to help the concerned educator: survey instruments, checklists, rating scales, and a variety of direct observation measures and procedures.

As an initial step in the assessment of the school and classroom context, administrators may want to survey critical stakeholders (e.g., teachers, parents, and students) to gather their opinions and beliefs about the school environment. Fraser (1999) discusses a number of specific instruments for assessing students' perceptions of classroom learning environments. For example, the *Individualized Classroom Environment Questionnaire* (ICEQ; Fraser, 1990) contains 50 Likert-scale items (e.g., The teacher takes personal interest in each student) to assess the attitudes of students in middle and high school across domains. The *Questionnaire on Teacher Interaction* (QTI; Goh & Fraser, 1996) contains 77 items (e.g., Is this teacher someone we can depend on?) to assess the nature and quality of the interaction between teachers and students. Teachers too can provide information related to the quality of the school climate. The *School-Level Environment Questionnaire* (SLEQ; Rentoul & Fraser, 1983) explores teachers' perceptions of the psychosocial dimensions of the environment of the school. The 56 items (e.g., I feel that I could rely on my colleagues for assistance should I need it) rate the school environment on eight dimensions.

Assessing parental attitudes toward school climate can be enlightening. For example, the Houston Independent School District (HISD), as part of its school reform efforts, developed and administered surveys to students, parents, and community members. The *HISD Parent Survey* (Stevens & Sanchez, 1999) has 44 items and the companion *HISD Community Survey* (Stevens & Sanchez, 1999) has 24 items. Both measures assess attitudes, beliefs, and opinions regarding the school's instructional environment, instructional processes, communication, administration, connectedness to the community, and security.

Direct observation of the school environment and the interactions that take place in various social contexts can provide additional information for identifying contextual strengths and weaknesses. Direct observation can be nonsystematic or systematic (Bakeman & Gottman, 1997). Nonsystematic observation involves collecting data without first developing specific codes or specifying operationally defined targets for observation. Information is typically gathered through anecdotal notes. Systematic observation involves developing specific behaviors that have been operationally defined and generally follows a specified method of data collection or behavioral sampling (e.g., Momentary Time Sampling; see Bakeman & Gottman, 1997, for a discussion of data collection procedures). Researchers and educators can use Tables 1 and 2 as guides for constructing checklists, surveys, and protocols for directly observing the school and classroom environment.

Checklists and or guided observation formats can be employed during direct observation to collect both formal and informal data. These measures typically assess the implementation of effective schools and teacher behaviors such as planning, management, instruction, and evaluation. Sample teacher observation systems include the Florida Performance Measurement System (Smith, 1985), the Classroom Snapshot (Stallings, 1980), and the Virginia Teacher Behavior Inventory (Teddlie, Virgilio, & Oescher, 1990).

Numerous empirically validated measures and procedures are available for educators to use when conducting a functional behavioral assessment of the school or classroom setting. As in efforts to gain a better understanding of an individual child's behavior, data gathered to explore the function of a behavior characteristic of a classroom or a school should be validated. The triangulation of data–that is, the identification of three independent sources of data (e.g., student survey, teacher checklist, and direct observation of the classroom setting) that indicate the same concern and the same function being served–is important. Educators should engage in a variety of procedures to gain a better understanding of their own teacher behavior (e.g., self- or peer-monitoring, teacher reflection). Additionally, school administrators should collect data to monitor the school context and to evaluate schools' improvement (VanAcker, 2002).

AREAS IN NEED OF FUTURE RESEARCH

Although considerable research has explored the school context in an effort to identify risk factors contributing to school failure and antisocial behavior, research to guide educators in ways to implement important and sustained change in teacher behavior is in shorter supply (Hall &

George, 1999). School environments can be very difficult to change. Lack of planning time, failure to develop a cohesive plan for change, teacher resistance, and ineffective monitoring of teacher and student behavior all contribute to the problem of effecting and sustaining change.

Research to identify the factors that contribute to developing and maintaining educator behaviors that impede student success is sorely needed. In some cases, teachers may be unaware of their behavior and its impact on student outcomes. For example, VanAcker and his colleagues (1996) found that teachers felt they were consistent in their delivery of praise and reprimand and were totally unaware of the differential distribution and contingent use of praise and reprimand across students. Pelletier, Suguin-Levesque, and Legault (2002), in a study to explore teacher management style, report that the more pressure teachers perceive from administration, the less self-determined they become in their teaching. They tend to become more autocratic and controlling with their students. Research that helps identify the social factors that bring about and maintain undesired features in the social environment of the school would be helpful.

Even when ineffective practices and behaviors are identified along with factors that support these behaviors, little empirical research targets direct and sustained change in teacher, staff, and administrator behavior in a systematic effort to improve the social context of the school. Although the literature suggests practices to promote sustained change in the school environment in general and in teacher and administrator behavior specifically (e.g., Hester, 2002; VanAcker, 2002), few empirically validated procedures have been outlined. Similar to student behavior, much of the behavior of the adults in the school is learned. Thus, behaviors that impede student success can be unlearned (e.g., Sutherland & Wehby, 2001b). What is needed is a research base to guide school administrators in their efforts toward school reform.

CONCLUSION

The school and the classroom represent unique social settings for children and youth. Unlike most social settings, attendance at school is mandated. Because students are compelled to attend schools, it would be beneficial to develop systems to help educators identify classroom and school problems before they are exacerbated. These educators could also learn from schools and classrooms that possess attributes or engage in practices that promote student success and resilience and prevent student failure (Nettles, Mucherah, & Jones, 2000; Rutter, 1983). Schools must avoid what Epp and Watkinson (1997) refer to as "systemic violence"–institutional practices or procedures that harm individuals or groups by burdening them psychologically, mentally, culturally, spiritually, economically, or physically. Applied to education, it means practices and procedures that undermine safety and prevent student learning.

Few educators intentionally set out to impede student success. Still, schools and classrooms often encourage or support failure. Why do educators and other school staff engage in practices and behaviors that hinder student success? What could be the function of these behaviors? Not surprisingly, many of the undesired school and classroom practices and behaviors serve the same functions as undesired student behaviors (e.g., attention, escape/avoidance, power/control, peer affiliation, self-gratification/competence, and justice/revenge; Neel & Cessna, 1993). In fact, many common school and classroom policies inadvertently support these ineffective practices and behaviors. For example, the current demand for increased student achievement across grade levels has intensified many of the zero tolerance regulations and uniform codes of conduct with specified consequences within the school. Students who display disruptive behavior in the classroom are frequently removed (e.g., suspended) from the classroom. Although removal provides a successful crisis management approach, it may actually increase the frequency and magnitude of the problem.

Students often become disruptive when they are unable to perform or are unsure of what is demanded within the classroom setting. By becoming disruptive and being removed, the student avoids (at least temporarily) the undesirable task. Thus, the student is negatively reinforced for disruptive behavior. As the student becomes disruptive, this behavior becomes increasingly aversive to the teacher. By removing the student, the disruption is removed, and the teacher too is negatively reinforced. If the removal of the student is the sole consequence provided (as is often the case), the student who was already unprepared to meet the expectations of the classroom has now missed yet another day of instruction and may be even less prepared to successfully engage in the assigned task–thus increasing the probability of increased disruptive behavior. In a school visited recently by one of the authors, one student had been suspended from school on 31 occasions for being disruptive in class. How can school staff hold any expectation that this student will be able to effectively engage in the classroom instruction after being removed from that setting so frequently?

Shores, Gunter, and their colleagues (Gunter, Denny, Shores, Reed, Jack, & Nelson, 1994; Shores, Gunter, & Jack, 1993) describe what they call the "curriculum of non-instruction." If a student becomes disruptive when given a task demand, the teacher may soon begin (consciously or unconsciously) to reduce the level of task demand to remove the potential for further disruption. Ultimately, the teacher and the student arrive at a situation in which the student covertly "agrees not to disrupt the learning" and the teacher "agrees not to challenge the student." Again, the teacher avoids undesired student behavior. Likewise, a teacher may inadvertently fail to provide an adequate level of instruction or opportunities to respond for students who lack the ability to pick up a given lesson or skill quickly in favor of calling on the brighter students. Thus, the teacher is more readily reinforced for his or her teaching, increasing his or her sense of competence and self-gratification.

Teaching is a very complex task. It is doubtful that a teacher could instruct a group of 24 to 28 diverse students throughout the course of the day without engaging in some excellent instructional behaviors as well as making numerous blunders. Nevertheless, because the goal is to promote student success, teachers develop and deliver quality instructional programs designed to "trap" their diverse student population into success. Teachers must strategically use the curriculum and themselves as agents of instruction. Educators need to implement practices that track student diversity and to develop lessons that take advantage of diversity. Therefore, a conscious effort to monitor teacher and student interaction is needed (VanAcker, 2002).

Although teachers are essential to school improvement, they do not work in isolation. Administrative leadership is vital. As Fullan and Hargreaves (1996, p. 87) state, "When a school has one or two bad teachers, this is usually a problem with the individual teacher. When it has many bad teachers, it is a problem of leadership." Further, programs that support students, other staff, and families as well as teachers must be in place (e.g., true collaboration, team- and co-teaching, thoughtful student-grouping strategies, and reasonable class size). Like individuals, school and classroom systems, when confronted with overwhelming challenges, may engage in behaviors that serve specific functions (e.g., avoidance or escape), which appear reasonable but lead to increased teacher and student failure and poor school performance and student violence (Mayer et al., 1983).

School improvement does require attention to individual warning signs. However, a focus on individual students alone will not produce safe and successful schools (Osher, Dwyer, & Jackson, 2003). Attention must also be paid to monitoring the school environment. Schools are dynamic, complex, ever changing. Different schools have different priorities, which reflect internal (e.g., student composition and needs) and external factors (e.g., budget crises and standards-based reform). School improvement should be considered a work in progress, subject to ongoing program modifications. These modifications should be based on objective data regarding

- students–how students are doing socially, emotionally, ethically, and academically; and
- school ecology–what school staff are doing to promote or undermine student development and what schools and districts are doing to promote or undermine effective practices and family school partnership.

These data can be employed to identify emerging problems, monitor success, and plan efficient interventions necessary to support appropriate behavior and academic success.

Schools that avoid examining data that help them address significant differences in learning and behaviors among children or are lax in giving teachers the support and professional consultation they need to attend to these individual differences will increase their risk for behavior problems. Schools that look for and address the why behind the observable behaviors and provide teachers and staff the team problem-solving support to develop effective interventions reduce their risk for the increased burdens that emotional and behavioral problems create (Batsche, 2000; Knoff & Batsche, 1995; Sugai & Horner, 1999).

REFERENCES

Bakeman, R., & Gottman, J. M. (1997). *Observing interaction: An introduction to sequential analysis.* Cambridge: Cambridge University Press.

Batsche, G. M. (2000). *Advanced workshop on facilitation of problem-solving teams and site-based evaluation of team performance.* National Association of School Psychologists annual conference, New Orleans, LA.

Beaman, R., & Wheldall, K. (2000). Teachers' use of approval and disapproval in the classroom. *Educational Psychology, 20*(4), 431-446.

Bellah, R. H., Sullivan, W. M., Tipton, S. M., Madsen, R., & Swidler, A. (1985). *Habits of the heart: Individualism and commitment in American life.* Berkeley, CA: University of California Press.

Brofenbrenner, U. (1977, July). Toward an experimental ecology of human development. *American Psychologist*, 513-531.

Brophy, J. (1988). Research on teacher effects: Uses and abuses. *Elementary School Journal*, *89*, 3-21.

Bryk, A. S., & Driscoll, M. E. (1988). *The school as community: Theoretical foundations, contextual influences, and consequences for students and teachers*. Madison, WI: National Center on Effective Secondary Schools.

Bryk, A. S., & Schneider, B. (2002). *Trust in schools: A core resource for improvement*. New York: Russell Sage Foundation.

Bryk, A. S., Lee, V. E., & Holland, P. B. (1993). *Catholic schools and the common good*. Cambridge, MA: Harvard University Press.

Cairns, R. B., Cairns, B. D., Neckerman, H. J., Gest, S., & Gariepy, J. L. (1988). Social networks and aggressive behavior: Peer support or peer rejection? *Developmental Psychology*, *24*, 815-823.

Catalano, R. F., Berglund, M. L., Ryan, J. A. M., Lonczak, H. S., & Hawkins, J. D. (2002). Positive youth development in the United States: Research findings on evaluations of positive youth development programs. *Prevention & Treatment*, *5*, Article 15. Retrieved May 15, 2003, from http://journals.apa.org/prevention/volume5/pre0050015a.html

Coie, J., Dodge, K., & Kupersmidt, J. B. (1990). Peer group behavior and social status. In S. R. Asher & J. D. Coie (Eds.), *Peer rejection in childhood* (pp. 17-59). Cambridge, GB: Cambridge University Press.

Conroy, M. A., & Fox, J. J. (1994). Setting events and challenging behaviors in the classroom: Incorporating contextual factors into effective intervention plans. *Preventing School Failure*, *38*(3), 29-34.

Crawford, L., Tindal, G., & Stieber, S. (2001). Using oral reading rate to predict student performance on statewide assessment tests. *Educational Assessment*, *7*(4), 303-323.

Dunn, E. K., & Eckert, T. L. (2002). Curriculum based measurement in reading: A comparison of similar versus challenging material. *School Psychology Quarterly*, *17*(1), 24-46.

Dwyer, K., & Osher, D. (2000). *Safeguarding our children: An action guide*. Washington, DC: U.S. Departments of Education and Justice, American Institutes for Research.

Dwyer, K., Osher, D., & Hoffman, C. C. (2000). Creating responsive schools: Contextualizing early warning, timely response. *Exceptional Children*, *66*(3), 347-365.

Dwyer, K., Osher, D., & Warger, C. (1998). *Early warning, timely response: A guide to safe schools*. Washington, DC: U.S. Department of Education.

Elliott, D. S., Grady, J. M., Shaw, T. E., Aultman-Bettridge, T., & Beaulieu, M. T. (2000). *Safe communities–safe schools planning guide: A tool for community violence prevention efforts*. Boulder, CO: Center for the Study and Prevention of Violence.

Epp, J. R., & Watkinson, A. M. (Eds.). (1997). *Systemic violence in education: Promise broken*. Albany, NY: State University of New York Press.

Epstein, J. L. (1995). School/family/community partnerships: Caring for the children we share. *Phi Delta Kappan*, *76*, 701-712.

Farmer, T. W., Farmer, E. M. Z., & Gut, D. M. (1999). Implications for social development research for school-based interventions for aggressive youth with EBD. *Journal of Emotional and Behavioral Disorders, 7*, 130-136.

Farmer, T. W., VanAcker, R., Pearl, R., & Rodkin, P. C. (1999). Social networks and peer-assessed problem behavior in elementary classrooms: Students with and without disabilities. *Remedial and Special Education, 20*(4), 244-256.

Felner, R. D. (2000). Educational reform as ecologically-based prevention and promotion: The project on high performance learning communities. In D. Cicchetti, J. Rappaport, I. Sandler, & R. P. Weissberg (Eds.), *The promotion of wellness in children and adolescents* (pp. 271-307). Washington, DC: CWLA Press.

Fox, J. J. (1990). Ecology, environmental arrangement, and setting events: An interbehavioral perspective on organizing settings for behavioral development. *Education and Treatment of Children, 13*(4), 364-373.

Fox, J. J., & Conroy, M. A. (1995). Setting events and behavioral disorders of children and youth: An interbehavioral field analysis for research and practice. *Journal of Emotional and Behavioral Disorders, 3*(3), 130-140.

Fraser, B. J. (1990). *Individualized classroom environment questionnaire.* Melbourne, AU: Australian Council for Educational Research.

Fraser, B. J. (1999). Using learning environment assessments to improve classroom and school climates. In H. J. Freiberg (Ed.), *School climate: Measuring, improving, and sustaining healthy learning environments* (pp. 48-64). Philadelphia: Falmer Press.

Fullan, M., & Hargreaves, A. (1996). *What's worth fighting for in your school.* New York: Teacher's College Press.

Furlong, M., & Morrison, G. (2000). The school in school violence: Definitions and facts. *Journal of Emotional and Behavioral Disorders, 8*, 71-82.

Goh, S. C., & Fraser, B. J. (1996). Validation of an elementary school version of the questionnaire on teacher interaction. *Psychological Reports, 79*, 515-522.

Gottfredson, G. D., & Gottfredson, D. C. (1985). *Victimization in schools.* New York: Plenum Press.

Greenberg, M. T., Weissberg, R. P., Utne O'Brien, M., Zins, J. E., Fredericks, L., Resnik, H., & Elias, M. J. (2003). Enhancing school-based prevention and youth development through coordinated social, emotional, and academic learning. *American Psychologist, 58*, 466-474.

Gunter, P. L., Denny, R. K., Shores, R. E., Reed, T. M., Jack, S. L., & Nelson, C. M. (1994). Teacher escape, avoidance, and countercontrol behaviors: Potential responses to disruptive behaviors of students with severe behavior disorders. *Journal of Child and Family Studies, 3*, 211-223.

Hall, G. E., & George, A. A. (1999). The impact of principal change facilitator style on school and classroom culture. In H. J. Freiberg (Ed.), *School climate: Measuring, improving, and sustaining healthy learning environments* (pp. 165-185). Philadelphia: Falmer Press.

Harter, S. (1999). *The construction of the self: A developmental perspective.* New York: Guilford.

Henderson, A. T., &. Mapp, K. L. (2002). *A new wave of evidence: The impact of school, family, and community connections on student achievement.* Austin, TX: Southwest Educational Development Laboratory.

Hester, P. (2002). What teachers can do to prevent behavior problems in schools. *Preventing School Failure, 47*(1), 33-38.

Hobbs, N. (1982). *The troubled & troubling child.* San Francisco: Jossey Bass.

Hulsebosch, P., & Logan, L. (1998). Breaking it up or breaking it down: Inner-city parents as co-constructors of school improvement. *Educational Horizons, 77*, 30-36.

Knoff, H. M., & Batsche, G. M. (1995). Project ACHIEVE: Analyzing a school reform process for at-risk and underachieving students. *School Psychology Review, 24*, 579-603.

Levering, B. (2000). Disappointment in teacher-student relationships. *Journal of Curriculum Studies, 32*(1), 65-74.

Lortie, D. C. (1975). *Schoolteacher.* Chicago: University of Chicago.

Mayer, G. R., Butterworth, T., Nafpaktitis, M., & Sulzer-Azaroff, B. (1983). Preventing school vandalism and increasing discipline: A three-year study. *Journal of Applied Behavior Analysis, 16*, 355-369.

McAfee, J. K. (1987). Classroom density and the aggressive behavior of children. *Education and Treatment of Children, 10*(2), 34-45.

Mc Andrews, T., & Anderson, W. (2002). *Schools within schools.* Washington, DC: U.S. Department of Education, Office of Educational Research and Improvement.

National Institute of Child Health and Human Development. (2002). The relation of global first-grade classroom environment to structural classroom features and teacher and student behavior. *Elementary School Journal, 102*(5), 367-387.

Neel, R. S., & Cessna, K. K. (1993). Behavioral intent: Instructional content for students with behavioral disorders. In K. K. Cessna (Ed.), *Instructionally differentiated programming: A needs-based approach for students with behavior disorders* (pp. 31-39). Denver, CO: Colorado Department of Education.

Nettles, S. M., Mucherah, W., & Jones, D. S. (2000). Understanding resilience: The role of social resources. *Journal of Education for Students Placed at Risk, 5*(1&2), 47-60.

Nias, J., Southworth, G., & Yeomans, R. (1989). *Staff relationships in the primary school.* London: Cassell.

Office of Educational Research. (1987). *Lesson structure: Research to practice.* ERIC Digest #448. Reston, VA: ERIC Clearinghouse on Handicapped and Gifted Students.

Osher, D. (1996). From supporting families to family friendly to collaborating with families: Metaphors, change, and service provision. *Proceeding of the National Conference on Research and Programs in Support of Children and Their Families* (pp. 166-170). Portland, OR: Portland State University.

Osher, D. (2000). Breaking the cultural disconnect: Working with families to improve outcomes for students placed at risk of school failure. In I. Ira Goldenberg (Ed.), *Urban education: Possibilities and challenges confronting colleges of education* (pp. 4-11). Miami, FL: Florida International University.

Osher, D., Dwyer, K., & Jackson, S. (2003). *Safe, supportive, and successful schools step by step.* Longmont, CO: Sopris West.

Osher, D., Kendziora, K. T., VanDenBerg, J., & Dennis, K. (1999). Beyond individual resilience. *Reaching Today's Youth, 3*(4), 2-4.

Osher, D., Morrison, G., & Bailey, W. (2003). Exploring the relationship between students: Mobility and dropout among students with emotional and behavioral disorders. *Journal of Negro Education, 72*(1), 79-96.

Osher, D., Quinn, M. M., Poirer, J. R., & Rutherford, R. (2003). Deconstructing the pipeline: Using efficacy and effectiveness data and cost-benefit analyses to reduce minority youth incarceration. *New Directions in Youth Development, 99*, 91-120.

Osher, D., Sandler, S., & Nelson, C. (Winter, 2001). The best approach to safety is to fix schools and support children and staff. *New Directions in Youth Development, 92*, 127-154.

Ostroff, C. (1992). The relationship between satisfaction, attitudes and performance: An organizational level analysis. *Journal of Applied Psychology, 77*(6), 963-974.

Pelleitier, L. G., Seguin-Levesque, C., & Legault, L. (2002). Pressure from above and pressure from below as determinants of teacher motivation and teaching behaviors. *Journal of Educational Psychology, 94*(1), 186-196.

Porter, A., & Brophy, J. (1988). Synthesis of research on good teaching: Insights from the work of the institute for research on teaching. *Educational Leadership, 45*(8), 74-85.

Quinn, M. M., Osher, D., Hoffman, C. C., & Hanley, T. V. (1998). *Safe, drug-free, and effective schools for ALL students: What works!* Washington, DC: American Institutes for Research, Center for Effective Collaboration and Practice.

Ratcliff, N. (2001). Use the environment to prevent discipline problems and support learning. *Young Children, 56*(5), 84-88.

Rentoul, A. J., & Fraser, B. J. (1983). Development of a school-level environment questionnaire. *Journal of Educational Administration, 21*, 21-39.

Repp, A. C. (1994). Comments on functional analysis procedures for school-based behavior problems. *Journal of Applied Behavior Analysis, 27*(2), 409-411.

Reynolds, D., & Teddlie, C. (2000). The process of school effectiveness. In C. Teddlie & D. Reynolds (Eds.), *The international handbook of school effectiveness research.* London: Falmer Press.

Reynolds, D., Teddlie, C., Creemers, B., Scheerens, J., & Townsend, T. (2000). An introduction to school effectiveness research. In C. Teddlie & D. Reynolds (Eds.), *The international handbook of school effectiveness research* (pp. 3-25). London: Falmer Press.

Rodkin, P., Farmer, T. W., Pearl, R., & VanAcker, R. (2000). Heterogeneity of popular boys: Antisocial and prosocial configurations. *Developmental Psychology, 36*(1), 14-24.

Rosenholtz, S. (1989). *Teacher's workplace: The social organization of schools.* New York: Longman.

Rutter, M. (1983). School effects on pupil progress. Research finding and policy implications. *Child Development, 54*, 1-29.

Ryan, W. F. (1972). *Blaming the victim.* New York: Vintage.

Sasso, G. M., Peck, J., & Garrison-Harrell, L. (1998). Social interaction setting events: Experimental analysis of contextual variables. *Behavioral Disorders, 24*(1), 34-43.

Shores, R. E., Gunter, P. L., & Jack, S. L. (1993). Classroom management strategies: Are they setting events for coercion? *Behavioral Disorders, 18*, 92-102.

Slavin, R. (1989). *School and classroom organization.* Mahwah, NJ: Erlbaum.

Smey-Richman, B. (1991). *School climate and restructuring for low-achieving students.* Philadelphia: Research for Better Schools.

Smith, B. O. (1985). Research bases for teacher education. *Phi Delta Kappan, 66*, 685-690.

Snyder, J., Morrison, G. M., & Smith, R. C. (1996). *Dare to dream: Educational guidance for excellence.* Indianapolis, IN: Lilly Endowment.

Stallings, J. A. (1980). Allocated academic learning time revisited. Or beyond time on task. *Educational Researcher, 2*, 11-16.

Stevens, C. J., & Sanchez, K. S. (1999). Perceptions of parents and community members as a measure of school climate. In H. J. Freiberg (Ed.), *School climate: Measuring, improving, and sustaining healthy learning environments* (pp. 124-147). Philadelphia: Falmer Press.

Sugai, G., & Horner, R. H. (1999). Discipline and behavior support: Preferred processes and practices. *Effective School Practices, 17*(4), 10-22.

Sugai, G., & Horner, R. H. (2002). Introduction to the special series on positive behavioral support in schools. *Journal of Emotional and Behavioral Disorders, 10*(3), 130-135.

Sugai, G., & Lewis, T. J. (1996). Preferred and promising practices for social skills instruction. *Focus on Exceptional Children, 29*(4), 1-16.

Sugai, G., Sprague, J. R., Horner, R. H., & Walker, H. M. (2000). Preventing school violence: The use of office discipline referrals to assess and monitor school-wide discipline interventions. *Journal of Emotional and Behavioral Disorders, 8*, 94-101.

Sutherland, K. S. (2000). Promoting positive interactions between teachers and students with emotional/behavioral disorders. *Preventing School Failure, 44*(3), 10-15.

Sutherland, K. S., & Wehby, J. H. (2001a). Exploring the relationship between increased opportunities to respond to academic requests and the academic and behavioral outcomes of students with EBD. *Remedial and Special Education, 22*(2), 113-121.

Sutherland, K. S., & Wehby, J. H. (2001b). The effect of self-evaluation on teaching behavior in classrooms for students with emotional and behavioral disorders. *Journal of Special Education, 35*(3), 61-71.

Teddlie, C., Virgilio, I., & Oescher, J. (1990). Development and validation of the Virginia Teacher Behavior Inventory. *Educational and Psychological Measurement, 50*(2), 421-430.

Tolan, P., & Guerra, N. (1994). *What works in reducing adolescent violence: An empirical review of the field.* Boulder, CO: Institute for Behavioral Science.

VanAcker, R. (2002). Establishing and monitoring a school and classroom climate that promotes desired behavior and academic achievement. In J. Chapple & L. M. Bullock (Eds.), *CASE/CCBD mini-library series: Safe, drug-free, and effective schools.* Arlington, VA: Council for Exceptional Children.

VanAcker, R., Grant, S., & Henry, D. (1996). Teacher and student behavior as a function of risk for aggression. *Education and Treatment of Children, 19*(3), 316-334.

Wagner, C. L., & Rutherford R. B. Jr. (1996). Social skills instruction: An essential component for learning. *Preventing School Failure, 41*(1), 20-23.

Wilson, D. B., Gottfredson, D. C., & Najaka, S. S. (2001). School-based prevention of problem behaviors: A meta-analysis. *Journal of Quantitative Criminology, 17,* 247-272.

Xie, H., Cairns, B. D., & Cairns, R. B. (1999). Social networks and configurations in inner-city schools: Aggression, popularity, and implications for students with EBD. *Journal of Emotional and Behavioral Disorders, 7*(3), 147-55.

Using Office Referral Records in School Violence Research: Possibilities and Limitations

Gale M. Morrison
Reece Peterson
Stacy O'Farrell
Megan Redding

SUMMARY. Perhaps the most "naturally occurring" data on school misbehavior and aggression are school discipline data, including office referrals, suspensions, and expulsion data. These data constitute the most common markers of school discipline status available on school campuses. There is, however, very little information available in professional or research literature about the reliability and validity of office referrals. This article examines the sources of error that enter into the

---

Gale M. Morrison is affiliated with The University of California, Santa Barbara, Gevirtz Graduate School of Education, Santa Barbara, CA 93106 (E-mail: gale@education.ucsb.edu).

Reece Peterson is affiliated with the University of Nebraska-Lincoln, Special Education, 202A Barkley Center, Lincoln, NE 68588-0732.

Stacy O'Farrell and Megan Redding are affiliated with the University of California, Santa Barbara, Gevirtz Graduate School of Education, Santa Barbara, CA 93106.

Address correspondence to Gale M. Morrison.

Data presented in this article were collected through support from a field-initiated research grant from the U.S. Department of Education, Special Education Programs, Grant #H324C000072.

[Haworth co-indexing entry note]: "Using Office Referral Records in School Violence Research: Possibilities and Limitations." Morrison, Gale M. et al. Co-published simultaneously in *Journal of School Violence* (The Haworth Press, Inc.) Vol. 3, No. 2/3, 2004, pp. 39-61; and: *Issues in School Violence Research* (ed: Michael J. Furlong et al.) The Haworth Press, Inc., 2004, pp. 39-61. Single or multiple copies of this article are available for a fee from The Haworth Document Delivery Service [1-800-HAWORTH, 9:00 a.m. - 5:00 p.m. (EST). E-mail address: docdelivery@haworthpress.com].

http://www.haworthpress.com/web/JSV
© 2004 by The Haworth Press, Inc. All rights reserved.
Digital Object Identifier: 10.1300/J202v03n02_04

collection and use of office referrals. Despite these sources of errors, this article documents the importance of considering how office referral data provide information about how discipline systems are functioning on a school campus. Guidelines are provided for utilizing disciplinary data for school safety and school policy planning. *[Article copies available for a fee from The Haworth Document Delivery Service: 1-800-HAWORTH. E-mail address: <docdelivery@haworthpress.com> Website: <http://www.HaworthPress.com> © 2004 by The Haworth Press, Inc. All rights reserved.]*

KEYWORDS. Office referrals, school violence, expulsion data, school discipline, school misbehavior

INTRODUCTION

What is the measure of a safe school? The federal and state governments have chosen to take a deficit approach and identify "persistently dangerous" schools. According to the federal No Child Left Behind Act (NCLB), states must develop and implement the Unsafe School Choice Option, which allows students to transfer to a "safe" public school if they are victims of violent crimes while on public school campuses or attend "persistently dangerous" schools. States are currently developing their guidelines. As an example, California has defined "persistently dangerous" schools as those that for three consecutive fiscal years have had a violent criminal offense committed on school property or have expelled students for one of nine violence-related offenses (e.g., assault, weapon possession, selling drugs).

Yet, as school safety efforts have developed over the past 10 to 15 years, safety has come to be defined as more than lack of weapon possession or physical assaults on campuses (Morrison, Furlong, & Morrison, 1994; Skiba et al., 2001). It also includes the absence of lower levels of violence on campus such as bullying, harassment, and ostracizing actions. Researchers have identified the most frequent disciplinary violations as lower levels of aggression and rule breaking such as tardiness, truancy and physical altercations between students (Heaviside, Rowand, Williams, & Farris, 1998; Skiba, Peterson, & Williams, 1997). Menacker, Hurwitz, and Weldon (1988) noted that defying authority was the most frequent offense, accounting for 23.4% of all offenses in one school year. In two recent *Los Angeles* (LA) *Times* articles on California's designation of "persistently dangerous" schools, concerns were raised about the high threshold created for designation as an unsafe school (Helfand, 2003; Helfand, Hayasaki, & DiMassa, 2003). One LA Unified School District official commented on how having such a high threshold for "dangerous" diverted attention from lower levels of disruption and violence. "If I've got fistfights on playgrounds, that's an important indication to me that we've got to do something" (Helfand, 2003). Thus, a more appropriate measure of school violence than severe dangerous actions would be the number of aggressive or disruptive actions that occur on campuses. While expulsion data may offer a general index of the most severe behavior, office referral data come closest to providing information about the day-to-day behavior on a school campus.

Exploration of the predictive validity of office referrals has concentrated primarily on the prediction of violent and delinquent behavior. Some researchers suggest that school discipline problems are a relatively good predictor of delinquency and aggressive behavior (Sprague, Walker, Stieber, Simonsen, & Nishioka, 2001; Tobin & Sugai, 1999) and therefore could be an important indicator of the potential for violence on a school campus. However, Sprague et al. note that correlations between office referral indices and delinquency range from low to moderate, indicating that there is much that remains to be understood about the specific patterns that may be represented within an overall index. Nelson, Benner, Reid, Epstein, and Currin (2002) suggested that the use of referral numbers as a screening tool for identification of students experiencing emotional and behavioral problems led to a large number of false negatives. Nelson and his colleagues also concluded from an overview of research literature that administrative referrals had limited predictive validity, as the more severe behaviors, those that go beyond the action of office referral, were most predictive of subsequent violent behavior (Nelson, Gonzalez, Epstein, & Benner, 2003). Since office referral data have become a common indicator for changes in schoolwide discipline patterns, understanding the technical adequacy of such an approach is critical in order to provide guidance in how best to use that information (Safran & Oswald, 2003).

The value of office referral data, while limited in terms of a prediction of extreme aggressive or violent behavior in its primary use for milder forms of school disruption, may rest in the ability to describe the day-to-day behaviors that detract from the overall safety of a school campus. For example, in addition to physical safety, developmental safety needs to be considered (Morrison et al., 1994); the ability of students to develop and learn in an environment that is safe from threat of harm, harassment or humiliation. Developmental safety addresses how school policies and the actions of school personnel affect students (Epp & Watkinson, 1997; Gottfredson & Gottfredson, 2001; Reinke & Herman, 2002). Office referral data may provide information about how schools are dealing with misbehavior, including the consistency and tone with which discipline is implemented. In this case, office referrals act as an indicator of the school's response to the student, in addition to an index of student behavior (Metzler, Biglan, Rusby, & Sprague, 2001); thus, the utility of office referrals as an indicator of system response is also the weakness of the indicator as a predictor of extreme forms of behavior.

Any analysis of office referrals as an "indicator" should recognize the multiple purposes for which these referrals can be used. One purpose is as a reflection of actual behavior exhibited on school campuses, leading to the temptation to predict future behavior from these data. The other purpose is to examine the systemic response to behaviors to test changes in behavior as a response to these changes. A third purpose relates to the potential use of office referral data to examine the *process* of school discipline that is practiced within individual schools. This purpose relates less directly to the prediction of future behavior, but is not totally removed from this prediction in the sense that exposing the process of a school's discipline system reveals the climate or context for student behavior. The following analysis explores the utility of office referrals for all of these purposes. While office referrals will be demonstrated to have multiple sources of error, these data may provide a rich source of information about discipline practices. Therefore, we will highlight the potential of these data to guide intervention with regard to school staff management practices and discipline policy.

Source of Observations and Illustrations

In order to illustrate the points made in this article, observations and data from a recently completed, federally supported research project, called *Turning Points*, designed to examine the school discipline trajectories of a sample of high-risk youth (with and without special education needs) will be presented.[1] This investigation took place in two districts, in schools serving predominantly Latino students from low socioeconomic neighborhoods. Over two hundred students (4th through 7th grade in the first year of the project) nominated by school personnel as experiencing school discipline problems were followed over a three-year period of time (2000-2003) to examine their academic and behavioral trajectories. The observations and data described in this article include information gathered at the school level at participating elementary schools during the process of gathering office referral data from school offices. Information presented is not intended to formulate conclusions or critique practices at participating schools, but rather to illustrate the points being made with regard to variation in office referral practice.

OFFICE REFERRAL DATA: AN ANALYSIS

Office referral data have been the focus of research as a tool for predicting later problem behavior and as a way of documenting improvements in school-wide discipline practices. Sugai, Sprague, Horner, and Walker (2000) defined office discipline referral as "an event in which (a) a student engaged in a behavior that violated a rule or social norm in the school, (b) the problem behavior was observed or identified by a member of the school staff, and (c) the event resulted in a consequence delivered by administrative staff who produced a permanent (written) product defining the whole event" (p. 96).

Patterns of Office Referral Numbers

As background, we present an example of the numbers of office referrals and suspensions administered during one academic year in eight elementary schools in two communities participating in the *Turning Points* project. Table 1 displays summary information about the size and nature of the school population, office referrals, and suspensions, demonstrating the type of variability in office referral and suspension data that might occur within and between districts. First, there are obvious size differences between the schools with unclear impact on the number of disciplinary actions, thereby limiting the use of these data without accounting for school size. Therefore, adjusting for school size, Figure 1 displays the ratios of office referrals to the school populations (*Mean* = .44) and the ratios of suspensions to the school populations (*Mean* = .08). These ratios should not be mistaken for the percentages of the school populations that are disciplined because the total numbers of office referrals or suspensions include duplicate offenses by the same students.

Within District 1 and 2, there is obvious differential use of office referrals and suspensions. As in RaffaeleMendez, Knoff, and Ferron (2002), not all schools with a high percentage of minority students or students receiving free and reduced lunches had equally high disciplinary rates, as all of these schools had relatively high representation from high need and minority populations. Of interest here are the patterns of

TABLE 1. Student Population, Demographic and Discipline Figures for Eight Elementary Schools

	District A				District B			
	School 1	School 2	School 3	School 4	School 5	School 6	School 7	School 8
Total population	806	870	784	642	571	629	803	494
% Free and Reduced Lunches	89.5	86.1	87.0	68.1	82.5	80.9	83.50	80.20
% English Language Learners	56.7	59.7	71.2	48.9	65	55.3	63.30	62.60
% Latino	96.1	86.6	97.7	75.2	94.2	87.3	95.50	93.10
# of office referrals	212	190	69	303	135	672	187	70
# of suspensions	21	45	30	9	2	19	26	6
Ratio: office referrals/school population	.263	.218	.881	.472	.236	1.07	.233	.142
Ratio: suspensions/school population	.026	.052	.038	.014	.004	.030	.032	.012

use of office referrals and suspensions adjusted for school size and compared with the averages for this group of schools. Schools 2 and 7 show higher than average use of suspensions and lower than average use of office referrals. In contrast, Schools 3 and 6 show the opposite pattern, high office referrals and low suspensions. In fact, School 6 had more office referrals than students in the school (again, the caveat that the office referrals included multiple offenses by individual students applies here).

There are a number of possible explanations for different patterns of disciplinary method use. For schools that have relatively high suspension rates but low office referral rates, it is possible that a zero-tolerance approach to discipline had been adopted. Students sent to the principal's office might have been greeted with an inflexible system of consequences for misbehavior. Alternatively, teachers might send students to the office for only the most serious offenses, indicating that they were able and willing to manage minor problem behaviors. Then, the students that did arrive in the office would do so having committed more serious offenses. However, the latter explanation implies that if the standard for suspension is used similarly across all schools, then Schools 2 and 7 have more students who commit suspendable offenses. Informal observations of these schools did not suggest that this is a viable hypothesis.

For schools that have a relatively high office referral rate and a low suspension rate, the office referral system possibly reflects a practice of sending students out of the classroom for minor incidents that do not reach the threshold for suspension. This explanation is illustrated by the nature of some of the office referrals made at these schools, which included the more traditional categories of fighting and disobedience, but also including disruptive mischievous behavior and academic noncom-

FIGURE 1. Ratios of Office Referrals and Suspensions to Respective School Populations

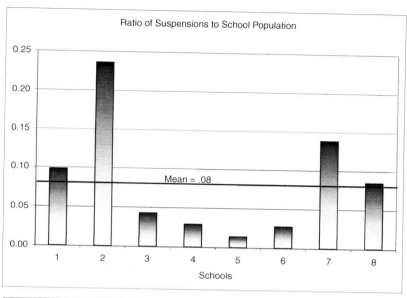

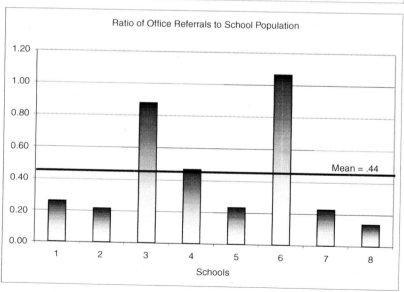

pliance: e.g., "She was cutting her hair with scissors" (kindergarten student). "Cheated on spelling test." "Play fighting." "Found Luis's pencil on the floor and kept it." "Mimicking the teacher." "Teasing 3rd graders." "Throwing raisins." These types of referrals may reflect any number of things, including a low teacher tolerance for misbehavior, lack of a systematic guide for school-wide discipline, or preference on the part of the principal to handle all misbehavior in the office in order to reduce distraction from academic tasks within the classrooms. With regard to low suspension rates, some elementary schools may simply not "believe" that suspension is appropriate for elementary school students.

Thus, there is a range of possible explanations for varied patterns of use of disciplinary measures in schools. These alternative hypotheses detract from the ability to use these data as valid and definitive indices of student behavior across schools. The different patterns seen within and between districts highlight the importance of closely examining the disciplinary practices at each school before making interpretations that align numbers with individual behavioral characteristics of students. However, understanding why these patterns exist could inform efforts to improve discipline practices in individual schools.

Office Referral Practices as Sources of Error in the Office Referral Measure

The following sections address common practices in the collection and use of office referral data. As Menacker et al. (1988) documented, there is extreme variability in record keeping with regard to school disciplinary actions, regardless of requirements set out by a systematic plan. Each practice will be examined for the sources of error that may detract from the reliability and validity of the office referral as a measure of school misbehavior.

Office Referral as a Process. There is no standardized instrument that constitutes an office referral. In the schools, each office referral is a process, which only sometimes has a written document associated with it. Generally the office referral process is simply the process wherein a teacher or other staff member sends a student to the office, presumably to meet with an administrator, presumably as a form of punishment for some action of the student.

A written document may or may not actually result from an office referral. Many elementary schools either do not use a formal office referral form or use such a form only for the most egregious behaviors. Our informal observations on the *Turning Points* project have indicated that students may spend a lot of time sitting in the office as a time-out for the teacher without an official office referral being made. Additionally, students are sometimes sent home for the remainder of the day without official notation. These practices may reflect that it has historically been easier at the elementary level to deal with behavior problems in the classroom, or on an informal basis with the administrator (Metzler et al., 2001).

Office Referral Forms. Office referral forms are the forms that some schools have developed to facilitate the process of school discipline. The office referral document, if there is one, is the way the sender knows that the student sees the administrator and that the administrator understands the reason for the referral. In some cases it is a way to keep track of information about this referral, particularly if the student is not able to see the administrator immediately. Commonly, the purpose of the form is to facilitate the process, not create a set of data.

The type of information included on the office referral form varies considerably from school to school but may include the following categories of information:

- Student name
- Grade
- Teacher
- Date of offense
- Location of offense
- Name of reporting adult
- Narrative description of offense
- Category of offense
- Narratives from witnesses
- Consequence or action taken
- Narrative apology or acknowledgement of offense by student
- Documentation of previous offenses
- Signature of student
- Signature of parent

Not all schools have a form, but may instead simply use a piece of paper, where the sender writes out a note. The following is an excerpt from a note sent to a principal from a teacher at the school, about an incident involving a group of boys who had gotten in trouble during lunch and were unresponsive to the supervisor on duty, and then rude to the office staff when the students were called in later. The excerpt demonstrates an additional purpose of an unstructured office referral note–to communicate about discipline policy.

> While the year is young, we must make an even bigger effort to ensure that these older, street-smart kids understand their need to be respectful to every adult on campus. Perhaps, for this grade level

of students, it is too much to ask the noontime supervisors to be out on the playground with so many, for so long on Mondays.

In schools with a formal office referral form, variations occur in terms of types of information collected and in format. For example, of eight elementary schools in the *Turning Points* research project, six had formal forms in use. Only one of these forms had a specific prompt to identify the *location* of the offense. Yet, as Astor and colleagues note (Astor, Meyer, & Behre, 1999), student perceptions of school violence are tied to specific locations on a school campus. Less supervised areas such as hallways and dining halls are perceived as particularly dangerous. By the very nature of being unsupervised, these locations are unlikely to have office referrals associated with them. Thus, using an index of office referrals as a measure of school safety would not represent all possible perspectives.

Among the elementary schools studied, two schools used multiple forms with regard to behavior. One of the schools had seven possible forms in use over a two-year period of time, four of these in use during any one year at the same time (these forms included four formats for student conduct at school, one for the bus, and two for reports home to parents). One of the these forms had three levels of behavior notations: a "green" level was for recognition of positive behavior, a "yellow" level was for offenses disciplined by the teacher, a "red" level was for offenses disciplined by an administrator. Each of these levels had four categories of behaviors: those relating to school safety, school climate, peer respect, and personal responsibility. The possible behaviors (check box provided for each) within the three levels and four general categories were 60. This was the most commonly used form; however, also popular was a form that had fewer choices and offered more room to describe a particular incident. At the same time that both of these forms were in use, the administrator kept a running record (multiple notations on each page) of students who visited the office, including information on the student name, the incident, the reporting adult, and the actions taken. This school also utilized student responsibility report forms and filed notes about the incident from teachers and students. There were some creative practices embedded within the multiple forms; however, between the number of forms and the changes in utilization between years, confusion among staff and disarray in the overall system was unavoidable. Clearly, attempting to get an unduplicated count of incidents was difficult, as multiple forms were utilized for any one situation.

In terms of how the incident is characterized on the office referral form, an important variation is how the misbehavior is framed, i.e., breaking rules and negative behavior or as a violation of a set of responsibilities or positive characteristics. In the case of School 4 in Table 1, the district had endorsed a school-wide character-building program, the "Character Counts" program (www.charactercounts.org), so the school changed their office referral form from listing five categories of negative behavior to reflect the specific "pillars of character." Instead of committing an offense, a student now "failed" to exhibit a "caring" pillar of behavior. Another school addressed responsibilities (as opposed to pillars of caring) on one form and rule violations on another form; both forms were in use at the same time. Framing misbehavior as the absence of positive rather than simply negative is an important philosophical difference in how communication and dialog around behavior occurs; the positive approach aligns with the emphasis on the best practice of positive behavior support and with a prevention-oriented philosophy (Bear, 1998; Safran & Oswald, 2003). However, while this office referral practice may align with what is considered best practices, the data from this school is likely less comparable to other schools who do not use a similar system.

These variations represent naturally occurring differences in practices, representing differing philosophies of school discipline, and would be considered a positive reflection of school creativity and ownership in implementation practices; however, these variations create a veritable nightmare for obtaining data that would be considered comparable across settings. Not only are such systems set up for collecting different sets of information, but the fidelity with which each school implements the system is frequently variable.

Terms Used on School Discipline Forms. For research and evaluation purposes, variations in the terminology used to describe student misbehavior on office referral forms may be problematic. There is clearly some question about the extent to which school data across forms that use different reporting categories are comparable. Even within a school using a single form, terminology remains a problem if terms are ambiguous or different staff members have differing interpretations of the terminology. Traditionally, little or no training is provided to most school staff members on how to complete school discipline forms, or on the meaning of the terms employed (Kingery & Coggeshall, 2001). For example a behavior such as "lack of cooperation" or "insubordination" may be listed, but no clear definition may exist in a school environment for that behavior. Even if there was a clearly intended definition, one teacher might be more lenient than another in interpreting the meaning of these behaviors (Wright & Dusek, 1998), creating problems of reliability in reporting.

Another caveat related to office referral terminology is citation of multiple offenses within one disciplinary referral. Examples from *Turning Points* include

> B. talks out of turn, disrupts others, and eats "hot cheetos" in class.

> J. has been here for one week, his behavior is undesirable, he yells, makes comments, lies, and is uncooperative. He lacks essential skills in academics.

While some forms permit the person filling it out to write a brief sentence or two of narrative description of the incident that might provide context, these are often not included in the data entry for computerized analysis, and this detail may be lost. Forcing incidents into specific terminology categories may limit the richness and complexity that is usually involved in an offense.

One final note is needed about discipline forms and their use. While the focus of the discussion about discipline forms has noted variation in practice that affect the reporting and numeration of incidents of misbehavior, in practice, there is another use for office referral forms, i.e., to record the consequence applied for the misbehavior. There is much variation in whether or not information about the consequence is solicited by the form. Additionally, practices noted on the *Turning Points* project include using the form as a parent contact mechanism, as a way of getting students to reflect on their actions, and as a student apology form or commitment to future improvement. These are example of how these forms are used for disciplinary practice; however, should information about the connection between consequences and behavior improvement be necessary, these variations would detract from accurate associations.

Error Associated with School Staff Training and Philosophy

In addition to referral process, systems, and forms, the reliability and validity of office referral data depends on the staff that are involved in implementing the system.

Teachers. Part of the error that may be generated in the process of disciplinary referral probably occurs at the classroom level. Teachers are generally highly variable in their ability to deal with problem behavior (Bear, 1998). There are variations in instructional effectiveness (which is related to problem behavior) (Scott, Nelson, & Liaupsin, 2001), classroom management abilities (Blankemeyer, Flannery, & Vazsonyi, 2002; Reinke & Herman, 2002), and tolerance levels for student activity and learning levels (Gerber, 1988; Wright & Dusek, 1998). Variability in teacher office referral rates may be less a measure of student behavior across classrooms and more an indicator of which teachers are struggling with their teaching and classroom management skills. The types of behaviors that would cause a student to be referred to the office in one classroom may be treated differently in another classroom, with in-class consequences such as time out, standing outside the classroom, or checks on the board leading to loss of privileges.

Indeed, an office referral may be more a reflection of the teacher's frustration level than the student's behavior. Bear (1988) suggests that the most common approach for disciplining the hostile aggressive, the defiant, and the passive aggressive student is control and suppression of undesirable behavior. Reimers, Wacker, and Koeppl (1987) note that teachers prefer strategies that are brief and simple to implement. These authors hypothesize that the appeal of controlling and punitive strategies lies in the ease of use and short-term effectiveness. For behaviors that are not responsive to teacher-utilized strategies, office referrals may be more a reflection or statement of the teacher's frustration level than the student's behavior. For example:

> Darin is on his 4th or 5th citation! He was in Mr. (teacher)'s yesterday and got a citation today! What are we to do with him? (Suspension?)

> Ivan has only turned his homework in twice. I talked to mom and she said she is a single mom and doesn't have time to help Ivan. I've taken away privileges but that doesn't work. I need help with this. Thanks, (teacher)

Vavrus and Cole (2002) made a similar point with regard to suspensions. Results of their qualitative study indicate that suspensions "are often preceded by a complex series of nonviolent events when one act among many is singled out for action by the teacher" (p. 87). In other words, it is not often the result of one single student engaging in physical or verbal abuse. The teacher must choose in a given moment who to single out for disciplinary action. The authors of this study contended that, in some cases, factors such as race and cultural background played into those choices.

From a teacher's perspective, the writing of an office referral often is influenced by the teacher's knowledge of what the administrator is likely to do with the student as a result of the referral. If the teacher believes that "nothing will happen" (no effective consequences), or that the punishment will be severe or harsh, the teacher may be less likely to write a referral (Mukuria, 2002). Conversely, should an administrator be seen for whatever the reason as being highly effective in working with referred students to get them to change their inappropriate behavior, the teachers may have an increased likelihood of writing office referrals. Either way the very existence of the referral depends on both the teachers' subjective experience and judgment about the administrator.

Teachers are often the thermometers for staff morale. Morrison and Skiba (2004) reported on differences between two consecutive years of office referrals at one school. During the second year, the office referrals for students using "profanity" nearly doubled. This could have been attributed to an upward trend in profanity use or to teachers' shortened fuses associated with their stress levels. As it happened, this school was undergoing a controversial change from a middle school format to a junior high format in order to ease the district finances.

Administrators. A great deal of the nature of the office referral system depends on the administrator who receives and deals with the referral. In elementary schools this often tends to be the principal along with the office secretary. The principal is a key person in setting the tone for discipline in the school, whether the general approach will be punitive and controlling or preventive in nature (Mukuria, 2002; Reimers et al., 1987). The principal as instructional leader also determines the extent to which the discipline system is systematic and consistently implemented. Sugai, Lewis-Palmer, Todd, and Horner (2001) outline criteria for judging the adequacy of a school-wide discipline program, which include the extent to which all staff agree on definitions of behavioral expectations, evidence of a system for responding to behavior (positive and rule-breaking), and evidence of use of data for decision making and management. The existence of these indicators requires leadership to ensure common agreement and appropriate training of all school staff. The principal is also the person who will generate funds and initiate for alternative disciplinary options such as in-school suspension, detention, trash pick-up, Saturday school, etc.

Principal practices have been associated with variations in discipline numbers (RaffaeleMendez et al., 2002; Skiba et al., 2003). At schools with lower suspension rates, administrators have designed and implemented strategies to reduce improper behavior; they have focused on prevention rather than punishment (RaffaeleMendez et al., 2002). Skiba et al. (2003) found that principal belief about discipline was reflected in the presence of the resources available on their campuses for prevention strategies and student support and development; those who believed in a zero tolerance approach to discipline and held negative attitudes toward special education and parents believed they had few resources and reported having fewer programs on their campuses. These attitudinal differences were reflected in the rate of suspensions at each of these schools; strict numerical comparisons of these schools could misrepresent the actual student behaviors.

Some administrators might come to view office referrals as a sign of poor teaching or behavior management skills. If such an attitude becomes known among teachers, it is likely that teachers will choose to deal with inappropriate behavior in ways other than through an office referral; the number of office referrals is likely to decline or remain low, compared to a building with a different attitude on this point.

Administrators receiving office referrals are primarily concerned with solving the student behavior problem, not necessarily in having accurate data. As a result, some administrators may alter the data that would have become an official office referral, perhaps even for purposes of effective intervention; for example, a promise to alter a disciplinary report in a student's record upon behavior improvement may be used as an incentive for student behavior change. While such a strategy may prove to be an effective intervention for encouraging students to take responsibility for their behavior, it argues against the reliability of office referrals as an accurate measure of overall student misbehavior. Administrators may also have certain offenses that they are extremely tough on, thereby having an "overrepresentation" of these offenses at their respective schools. While there may not truly be more of these offenses at their school, since they are keeping an eye out for these offenses, they may record more at their school than other administrators record at their respective schools.

Clearly, therefore, when a building administrator in charge of discipline changes positions, the system of discipline likely will change as well. Morrison and Skiba (2004) documented the significant change in suspension rate from one year to the next, where the likely cause was change of the principal of the school. RaffaeleMendez et al. (2002)

noted the same elevated suspension rates for high teacher turnover rates. Thus, changes in key administrative leadership should be tracked when comparing office referrals through time, even in one building.

Use of Office Referrals for Documenting Change in School-Wide Discipline Systems

Over the past 20 years, a variety of school-wide discipline systems and systems for positive behavioral support have been marketed to the schools (Safran & Oswald, 2003). Some schools have developed their own. One of the advantages of these systems is that they often foster communication across faculty, other staff and administration regarding appropriate and inappropriate behavior. They lead to discussions about when it is appropriate to write an office referral and what the categories of behavior on the form mean. It may also lead to an understanding of and perhaps more consistency in the repertoire of disciplinary responses for office referrals. It is difficult to come up with a "downside" to having a school-wide discipline program, unless the particular program is one that encourages negative or punitive consequences.

Office referral data are also being used as a measure of effectiveness of positive behavior support programs (Metzler et al., 2001; Sprague, Walker, Golly et al., 2001). Dramatic changes in the numbers of office referrals are being used to show the effect of implementing these programs. While worth tracking, during changes in policies or procedures related to behavior, office referrals are not necessarily a good dependent measure for indexing systems change. Changes in office referrals under these circumstances are more likely a combined product of improved consistency and understanding by staff and administrators, as well as actual changes in student behavior. In fact the number of office referrals could conceivably go up during the first year of implementation of a behavioral program. This can be readily understood if prior to the changes teachers felt that office referrals were ineffective and with a new system their usefulness has been improved. Conversely, in a school where discipline was poor and the number of office referrals was very high, a dramatic fall in the number of office referrals should probably not be taken as a result entirely of the particular program being implemented, as much as a result of a return to basic communication, and consistency around these issues. Here the decrease may simply be the result of teachers acknowledging their role in basic classroom management and striking a better balance in making office referrals. Certainly claims for immediate reduction of office referrals as a result of a new school-wide discipline program should be embraced cautiously. In order to confirm claims of behavior change, it is advisable to include independent measures, such as behavior rating scales and checklists or observational data, to corroborate office referral data.

Standardized Office Referral Data Systems

Most of the observations and comment about office referrals made so far in this paper have related to elementary schools. Secondary schools are larger by nature and have tend to have more formal discipline systems in place. Both as a result of these schools becoming larger, and therefore more bureaucratic, as well as new needs to track student behavior, the office referral form has become commonplace in most junior high and high schools. Increasing concerns about school violence and crime may also have quickened the pace towards a more formalized, more sophisticated system. This trend may also partly be a result of legal issues related to discipline, especially around issues such as student expression (*Tinker v. Des Moines*, 1969), use of corporal punishment (*Ingraham v. Wright*, 1997), and appropriateness of suspension (*Goss v. Lopez*, 1975). As a result of these and other decisions, a series of due process procedures have evolved around school discipline. One of the outcomes of these evolving legal standards is that accusations of misconduct must be related to a written code or policy. Thus, office referral forms have been revised in many schools to indicate offenses that are directly related to a district or school code of conduct. As a result of case law, state's legislation, and concerns for privacy, the discipline records (typically office referral forms and other records) for students are kept separate from the academic records of students.

As a result of some of the problems mentioned earlier regarding office referral data and in order to facilitate the answering of questions posed above, several commercial systems have been developed and marketed to address some of the problems. They typically create a computer database that can be used to generate various reports and charts of office referral data. Some are part of larger school management software systems available for purchase at the district level, and others are designed only for the office referral function. They vary in the degree to which a particular school can revise the structure or categories of the office referral form, and thus the degree to which they may be able to meet policy requirements related to codes of conduct. Some programs are installed and maintained locally, while others are Web based and permit a school to upload a data set for analysis and download the resulting reports. They also vary in the kinds of reports that can be generated. Some examples of these include (a) BoysTown (www.girlsandboystown.org/pros/training/education/index.asp), (b) Powerschool (www.apple.com/education/powerschool/), (c) The School Wide Information System (SWIS) (www.swis.org), and (d) Schoolmaster (www.schoolmaster.com).

While these may be a quick way for a school to get information for data analysis, the data entry still remains a local problem, and the costs of these programs may be a disincentive to their use. On the other hand, at least some of these systems provide definitions of behavior categories, and training materials for competing the forms.

One of the disadvantages of having office referral forms computerized is that many times they permit only one student behavior to be identified and entered in the database per incident, although multiple behaviors fitting multiple categories might have occurred in the incident. As result, the individual completing the form may be able to choose only one behavior, or if more than one are checked, the person entering the data may only be able to enter one. These kinds of arbitrary forced choices limit the richness, and perhaps the usefulness of the data. It may not be clear whether the offense picked is the most serious or most important of the offenses.

RECOMMENDATIONS, POSSIBILITIES, AND CONCLUSIONS

We have described the variation that occurs within the implementation of office referral systems. Error lies in the differing processes, forms, terminology, and staff philosophy and training. Because of this variation in school discipline systems, it is difficult to make meaningful comparisons across schools with regard to numbers of discipline referrals, as an offense at one school may not be recorded as an offense at anoher school. Alternative explanations can easily be generated for numbers of office referrals and resulting suspensions. Therefore, extreme caution is needed when interpreting and comparing school-wide totals for these indices. (Our focus here was primarily office referrals; suspension and expulsion process error have been described more extensively in Morrison and Skiba [2001] and Morrison et al. [2002].)

A discipline system will meet standards of fairness and consistency only if the individuals involved coordinate and communicate their understandings with each other. As a result, office referrals might be viewed as subjective, if not qualitative, data. Quantitative analysis of office referral data can lead to misinterpretations, unless the limitations and strengths of this type of data are clearly in mind during the analysis. The following recommendations are designed to address the use of office referral data for the purpose of characterizing and comparing schools in a quantitative fashion.

Recommendations

In order to address, on the one hand, the value of office referrals as naturalistic data in the environment, but in order also to acknowledge their limitations, the following are recommended for use of office referral data (not in sequence of priority):

1. Whenever office referral data are used to make between-school and longitudinal comparisons, the existence of the following should be documented:
   a. Changes in the building leadership team or district administration resulting in possibly different philosophies related to discipline;
   b. Existence of, or change in, a building or district-wide school discipline/behavior management program;
   c. Turnover rate of school staff during the time period of concern.
2. Due to difficulties with definition of terms and categorizing offenses, office referral data are probably more reliable for tracking the more serious and the more obvious offenses such as "fighting" or "having drugs at school" as compared to the more subjective offenses such as "being disruptive," "lack of cooperation" or "insubordination."
3. Comparing office referral data for the purpose of suggesting or implying differences in the amount or types of inappropriate behavior among students in different schools is difficult, as these differences may reflect differences in the systems or personnel, rather than differences in actual student behavior.
4. Use of office referral data is best when it is one element of a package of data sources about a school, which might include number of students suspended and the number of days of suspension, number of students expelled, and length of expulsion, number of absences and tardies, as well as staff and student perceptions regarding the degree of inappropriate student behavior.
5. Pre-post office referral data related to behavior intervention studies, whether for school-wide discipline or positive behavioral support implementation should be used cautiously since results may reflect changes in the data creation mechanism as much as changes in student behavior.

Possibilities

Office referral data, despite all of the limitations as a standardized assessment tool, have much to offer in the way of information. Although school-to-school and within school comparisons (across time) are unwise unless standard information about the types of information collected and fidelity of that collection are ensured, office referral data may provide informative data about discipline practices. Some of the following questions that could be asked of this information source may be useful in refining one's discipline and reporting system.

Who. Who are the students who repeatedly get sent to the office (grades, academic status, special education status, ethnicity, gender)?

Nature of Behavior. What is the nature of their misbehavior? Are there threshold behaviors that guarantee an office referral? Are there behaviors that are handled by some teachers in the classroom and by some with a referral out of the classroom? Is there a trend in the type of behavior exhibited that is related to fads or community trends (drugs, slang, sexual conduct)?

Location. In what campus locations are students getting in trouble?

Personnel Reactions. Who refers students most often (teachers, yard supervisors)? Would this misbehavior receive the same response in another classroom?

When. When (time of day) do students tend to get in trouble? What months/days of week are most likely to reap office referrals?

Effectiveness. What consequences seem to reduce office referrals? Do these consequences work differentially for different types of students? Is there a sequence of severity that works? Mild to severe or straight to severe?

Conclusion

In conclusion, we have highlighted the multiple sources of error that might creep into an office referral system, making the reliability and validity of those data suspect. These multiple sources of potential error in office referral data argue that they should be used with caution as a measurement tool. They must be recognized as representing a naturally occurring data source related to an important school function. They also represent the particular definitions and customs of a particular school and school district. They typically have not been designed for purposes of research, and may not have the technical characteristics desirable for purposes of quantitative research.

However, in addition to being a potential source of data for prediction, albeit limited according to the extent of standardization in its implementation, office referrals also may serve the purpose of providing a rich description of the process of school discipline practices. Office referrals, especially when they include narrative comment, provide a vivid picture of the human foibles and challenges in the day-to-day reality of schools. They can be an excellent indicator of the behavioral health of a school, but only if they are used cautiously, acknowledging the limitations of this type of data, and the peculiar system that they reflect.

NOTE

1. *Turning Point Effects for Students with and Without Disabilities Who Are Involved in School Disciplinary Actions;* grant awarded to the senior author by the U.S. Department of Education, Office of Special Education Programs, Award # H324C00007.

REFERENCES

Anderman, E. M., & Kimweli, D. M. (1997). Victimization and safety in schools serving early adolescents. *Journal of Early Adolescence, 17*(4), 408-438.

Astor, R., Meyer, H. A., & Behre, W. J. (1999). Unowned places and times: Maps and interviews about violence in high schools. *American Educational Research Journal, 3*(1), 3-42.

Bear, G. G. (1998). School discipline in the United States: Prevention, correction, and long-term social development. *Educational and Child Psychology, 15*(1), 15-39.

Blankemeyer, M., Flannery, D. J., & Vazsonyi, A. T. (2002). The role of aggression and social competence in children's perceptions of the child-teacher relationship. *Psychology in the Schools, 39*(3), 293-304.

Epp, J. R., & Watkinson, A. M. (Eds.). (1997). *Systemic violence in education: Promise broken.* Albany, NY: State University of New York Press.

Gerber, M. M. (1988). Tolerance and technology of instruction: Implications for special education reform. *Exceptional Children, 54*(4), 309-314.

Goss v. Lopez. (1975). 419 US 565.

Gottfredson, G. D., & Gottfredson, D. C. (2001). What schools do to prevent problem behavior and promote safe environments. *Journal of Educational and Psychological Consultation, 12*(4), 313-344.

Heaviside, S., Rowand, C., Williams, C., & Farris, E. (1998). *Violence and discipline problems in U.S. Public Schools: 1996-97* (No. NCES 98-030). Washington, DC: U.S. Department of Education, National Center for Education Statistics.

Helfand, D. (2003, July 8). School danger narrowly defined. *Los Angeles Times*, pp. 1, 11.

Helfand, D., Hayasaki, E., & DiMassa, C. M. (2003, July 10). No schools in state overly dangerous. *Los Angeles Times*, pp. 1, 12.

Ingraham v. Wright. (1997). 430 U.S. 651.

Kingery, P. M., & Coggeshall, M. B. (2001). Surveillance of school violence, injury, and disciplinary actions. *Psychology in the Schools, 38*, 117-126.

Menacker, J. C., Hurwitz, E., & Weldon, W. (1988). Legislating school discipline: The application of a systemwide discipline code to schools in a large urban district. *Urban Education, 23*, 12-23.

Metzler, C. W., Biglan, A., Rusby, J. C., & Sprague, J. R. (2001). Evaluation of a comprehensive behavior management program to improve school-wide positive behavior support. *Education and Treatment of Children, 24*(4), 448-479.

Morrison, G. M., Anthony, S., Storino, M. H., Cheng, J. J., Furlong, M. J., & Morrison, R. L. (2002). School expulsion as a process and an event: Before and after effects on children at risk for school discipline. In R. J. Skiba & G. G. Noam (Eds.) *Zero tolerance: Can suspension and expulsion keep school safe?* San Francisco: Jossey-Bass.

Morrison, G. M., Furlong, M. J., & Morrison, R. L. (1994). School violence to school safety: Reframing the issue for school psychologists. *School Psychology Review, 23*(2), 236-256.

Morrison, G. M., & Skiba, R. J. (2001). Predicting violence from school misbehavior. *Psychology in the Schools, 38*, 173-184.

Morrison, G. M., & Skiba, R. J. (2004). School discipline indices and school violence: An imperfect correspondence. In M. J. Furlong, M. P. Bates, D. C. Smith, & P. E. Kingery (Eds.), *Appraisal and prediction of school violence: Methods, issues, and contexts*. Hauppauge, NY: NovaScience Publishers.

Mukuria, G. (2002). Disciplinary challenges: How do principals address this dilemma? *Urban Education, 37*(3), 432-452.

Nelson, J. R., Benner, G. J., Reid, R. C., Epstein, M. H., & Currin, D. (2002). The convergent validity of office discipline referrals with the CBCL-TRF. *Journal of Emotional & Behavioral Disorders, 10*(3), 181-188.

Nelson, J. R., Gonzalez, J. E., Epstein, M. H., & Benner, G. J. (2003). Administrative discipline contacts: A review of the literature. *Behavioral Disorders, 2003*(3), 249-281.

RaffaeleMendez, L. M., Knoff, H. M., & Ferron, J. M. (2002). School demographic variables and out-of-school suspension rates: A quantitative and qualitative analysis of a large, ethnically diverse school district. *Psychology in the Schools, 39*(3), 259-277.

Reimers, T. M., Wacker, D. P., & Koeppl, G. (1987). Acceptability of behavioral interventions: A review of the literature. *School Psychology Review, 16*, 212-227.

Reinke, W. M., & Herman, K. C. (2002). Creating school environments that deter antisocial behaviors in youth. *Psychology in the Schools, 39*(5), 549-560.

Safran, S., & Oswald, K. (2003). Positive behavior supports: Can schools reshape disciplinary practices? *Exceptional Children, 69*(3), 361-373.

Scott, T., Nelson, C. M., & Liaupsin, C. J. (2001). Effective instruction: The forgotten component in preventing school violence. *Education and Treatment of Children, 24*(3), 309-322.

Skiba, R. J., Peterson, R., Miller, C., Boone, K., McKelvey, J., Fontanini, A. et al. (2001). The safe and responsive schools project: Comprehensive planning for school violence prevention. *Communique, 29*(7), 16.

Skiba, R. J., Peterson, R. L., & Williams, T. (1997). Office referrals and suspension: Disciplinary intervention in middle schools. *Education and Treatment of Children, 20,* 295-315.

Skiba, R. J., Simmons, A., Staudinger, L., Rausch, M., Dow, G., & Feggins, R. (2003). *Consistent removal: Contributions of school discipline to the school-prison pipeline.* Paper presented at the School-to-Prison Pipeline, Boston, MA.

Sprague, J., Walker, H., Golly, A., White, K., Myers, D. R., & Shannon, T. (2001). Translating research into effective practice: The effects of a universal staff and student intervention on indicators of discipline and school safety. *Education and Treatment of Children, 24*(4), 495-511.

Sprague, J., Walker, H. M., Stieber, S., Simonsen, B., & Nishioka, V. (2001). Exploring the relationship between school discipline referrals and delinquency. *Psychology in the Schools, 38*(2), 197-206.

Sugai, G., Lewis-Palmer, T., Todd, A. W., & Horner, R. H. (2001). *Systems-wide evaluation tool.* Eugene: University of Oregon.

Sugai, G., Sprague, J. R., Horner, R. H., & Walker, H. M. (2000). Preventing school violence: The use of office discipline referrals to assess and monitor school-wide discipline interventions. *Journal of Emotional and Behavioral Disorders, 8,* 94-101.

Tinker v. Des Moines Independent Community School District. (1969) 393 U.S. 503, 509.

Tobin, T., & Sugai, G. (1999). Using sixth-grade school records to predict school violence, chronic discipline problems, and high school outcomes. *Journal of Emotional and Behavioral Disorders, 7*(1), 40-53.

Vavrus, F., & Cole, K. (2002). "I didn't do nothing": The discursive construction of school suspension. *The Urban Review, 34*(2), 87-111.

Wright, J. A., & Dusek, J. B. (1998). Compiling school base rates for disruptive behaviors from student disciplinary referral data. *School Psychology Review, 27*(1), 138-147.

Identification of Bullies and Victims: A Comparison of Methods

Dewey G. Cornell

Karen Brockenbrough

SUMMARY. Bullying studies frequently rely on student self-report to identify bullies and victims of bullying, but research in the broader field of peer aggression makes greater use of other informants, especially peers, to identify aggressors and victims. This study compared self, peer, and teacher identification of bullies and bully victims in a sample of 416 middle school students. Overall, there was poor correspondence between self-reports and reports made by peers or teachers, but consistently better agreement between peers and teachers, in identifying both bullies and victims of bullying. Peer and teacher identification of bullies were more consistently associated with subsequent school disciplinary infractions than were self-reports. These results raise concern about reliance on student self-reports of bullying and bully victimization. *[Article copies available for a fee from The Haworth Document Delivery Service:*

Dewey G. Cornell, PhD, is affiliated with the Programs in Clinical and School Psychology, Curry School of Education, University of Virginia, 405 Emmet Street, Charlottesville, VA 22903-2495 (E-mail: dcornell@virginia.edu).

Karen Brockenbrough is affiliated with the Virginia Treatment Center for Children, 515 North 10th Street, PO Box 980489, Richmond, VA 23298-0489.

Address correspondence to Dewey G. Cornell.

The authors thank the staff and students of the middle school who participated in this project. They also thank staff members of the Virginia Youth Violence Project for assistance in data collection.

[Haworth co-indexing entry note]: "Identification of Bullies and Victims: A Comparison of Methods." Cornell. Dewey G., and Karen Brockenbrough. Co-published simultaneously in *Journal of School Violence* (The Haworth Press, Inc.) Vol. 3, No. 2/3, 2004, pp. 63-87; and: *Issues in School Violence Research* (ed: Michael J. Furlong et al.) The Haworth Press, Inc., 2004, pp. 63-87. Single or multiple copies of this article are available for a fee from The Haworth Document Delivery Service [1-800-HAWORTH. 9:00 a.m. - 5:00 p.m. (EST). E-mail address: docdelivery@haworthpress.com].

http://www.haworthpress.com/web/JSV
© 2004 by The Haworth Press, Inc. All rights reserved.
Digital Object Identifier: 10.1300/J202v03n02_05

1-800-HAWORTH. E-mail address: <docdelivery@haworthpress.com> Website: <http://www.HaworthPress.com> © 2004 by The Haworth Press, Inc. All rights reserved.]

KEYWORDS. Bullies, school violence, victims, middle school, aggressors

Student self-report surveys are the most common research method of identifying bullies and victims of bullies. National studies rely on self-report surveys to determine prevalence rates of bullying (Nansel, Overpeck, Pilla, Ruan, Simons-Morton, & Scheidt, 2001; Solberg & Olweus, 2003). Schools that undertake programs to reduce bullying are advised to rely on self-report surveys to measure the effectiveness of their efforts (Olweus, 1997; Olweus, Limber, & Mihalic, 1998). Nevertheless, we know little about the accuracy of student self-reports of bullying. Because such surveys are almost always administered on an anonymous basis, there is no means of linking student responses to independent, external sources of information that can confirm or disconfirm the student's report.[1]

In contrast, researchers in the closely related field of peer aggression rely less heavily on student self-report and make more frequent use of other informants in assessing a child's involvement as an aggressor or victim of peer aggression, such as peers, teachers, and parents. Perhaps the most common research method in peer aggression research is the use of peer reports, widely (but not universally) regarded as the gold standard for identifying victims of peer aggression (Ladd & Kochenderfer-Ladd, 2002; Perry, Kusel, & Perry, 1988). The peer report or peer nomination method typically involves surveying a classroom of students and asking each of them independently to identify classmates who match a descriptive statement, such as "someone who gets hit, pushed, or kicked by other kids" (Ladd & Kochenderfer-Ladd, 2002, p. 95). The number of times a student is nominated by peers is used as an index of the student's victim status, and a cutoff may be used to classify a student as a victim or non-victim. In some variations of this method, students are asked to assess their classmates on a series of descriptive statements, they may be asked to nominate a fixed number of classmates, or they may be asked to assign frequency ratings (e.g., never, sometimes, often) to each of their classmates.

Self-reports are by definition subjective and can be prone to biases that could lead to either over- or underreporting of victim experiences. With regard to bullying, students may be reluctant to acknowledge socially undesirable behavior such as bullying or being the victim of bullying. Peer reports are not without limitations and potential biases as well, but the aggregation of judgments across multiple informants offers some protection against bias and, according to psychometric principles, should produce more reliable results than judgments based on a single source or rating (Ladd & Kochenderfer-Ladd, 2002).

Several studies have supported the reliability and validity of peer-report measures of child victimization in middle and high school age children (Achenbach, McConaughy, & Howell, 1987; Ladd & Kochenderfer-Ladd, 2002; Nabuzoka, 2003; Perry et al., 1988). However, researchers have found only moderate correspondence between self- and peer reports, generally in the range of .14 to .42 (Achenbach et al., 1987; Ladd & Kochenderfer-Ladd, 2002; Perry et al., 1988).

Ladd and Kochenderfer-Ladd (2002) compared self- and peer reports of peer victimization in 197 children in grades K-4. Although their study was not concerned specifically with bullying, they examined student self-reports of being the victim of peer aggression, including physical, verbal, and social forms of aggression that correspond with the types of peer aggression included in most definitions of bullying. They found that concordance between self- and peer reports were virtually zero at the kindergarten level, but increased with age, and reached .50 among fourth grade students. In a follow-up study with 390 children in grades 2-4, Ladd and Kochenderfer-Ladd (2002) examined the concordance among self-, peer, and teacher report measures of child victimization. Once again they observed increasing levels of concordance in higher grades. For fourth-grade students, self-reports correlated .47 with peer reports and .30 with teacher reports, whereas peer and teacher reports correlated .47.

Solberg and Olweus (2003) strongly endorsed the use of self-report surveys to determine the prevalence of bullies and victims of bullying in schools, and argued against the use of peer nominations to assess the prevalence of bullying. In their study, students were administered a revised version of the Olweus Bully/Victim Questionnaire, and the survey was administered on an anonymous basis in school classrooms. The survey presented students with a standard definition of bullying, followed by a series of questions about the student's experience of being bullied or engaging in bullying behavior. Two key questions asked students to rate how frequently they had been bullied or had bullied others, and students who endorsed a frequency of "2 or 3 times a month" or more often were classified as victims or bullies, respectively.

Solberg and Olweus (2003) acknowledged the potential problems of under- and overreporting of bullying in self-report surveys, which they described as "a big and complex issue that cannot be treated satisfactorily within the scope of the present article" (p. 264). The researchers demonstrated that self-reported bullying was correlated with measures of externalizing behavior and that self-reported victimization was correlated with measures of internalizing behavior, but all data were obtained from the same questionnaire, supporting the consistency of student responses and not necessarily their accuracy. Questions of under- and overreporting of bullying cannot be answered without reference to external criteria independent of the student's self-report.

The purpose of the present study was to compare student self-reports of bullying and bully victimization with independent peer and teacher reports. We designed instruments for all three informant sources that used the same definition of bullying and asked informants parallel questions to identify bullies and bully victims. One barrier to research on bullying self-report surveys is that they are almost always administered on an anonymous basis, so that researchers have no means of comparing individual student responses with any external criteria. Consequently, in the present study we departed from the usual practice by administering the self-report surveys on a confidential, but not anonymous, basis.

We investigated two main study questions. First, we examined the correspondence between self-reported victimization and reports made by classmates and by teachers. We assessed the levels of agreement among these three sources using multiple cutoff points. We conducted parallel analyses for self-reported bullying and for the self-report of being a victim of bullying.

Second, we investigated the predictive validity of all three measures on subsequent student discipline referrals, detentions, and suspensions over the next seven months (the time period for which data were available). School records provide still another source of information independent of self-report, one that is incident based, cumulative, and prospective rather than based on a retrospective judgment. Based on previous studies and observations of bullies (e.g., Olweus, 1993, 1997; Smith, 1997), we hypothesized that bullies would be more likely than other students to be referred for disciplinary infractions and to receive consequences such as detentions and suspensions.

METHOD

Participants

The study was conducted in a middle school serving 581 students (grades 6-8) in a mixed rural and suburban area in central Virginia. Approximately 30% of the students received a free or reduced school lunch. Study participants were recruited by a letter asking both parents and their children for permission for the students to complete a confidential survey at school. Of the 581 students, 527 students (91%) returned their forms, 423 (73%) agreed to participate, and 416 (72%) ultimately completed the survey.

Of the 416 students who completed the survey, 49% were boys and 51% were girls. Thirty-four percent of the participants were in the sixth grade, 35% were in the seventh grade, and 31% in the eighth grade. Participant ages ranged from 10 to 14. Seventy-eight percent of the participants identified themselves as Caucasian, 12.3% as African-American, 3.9% as Hispanic, 2.4% as Asian-American, 1.0% as Native American, and 1.9% as Other.

Measures

Students completed the *School Climate Survey*, a 77-item self-report survey compiled by the authors using items and scales from previous instruments. The full survey included scales to measure involvement in bullying behaviors and attitudes toward bullying, as well as more general feelings about school, self-concept, recent grades, and discipline history, as described in detail elsewhere (Brockenbrough, 2001); in this study, we were concerned only with items intended to identify bullies and victims.

The survey presented students with the following definition of bullying:

> We say someone is bullying when he or she hits, kicks, grabs, or shoves you on purpose. It is also bullying when a student threatens or teases you in a hurtful way. It is also bullying when a student tries to keep others from being your friend or from letting you join in what they are doing. It is not bullying when two students of about the same strength argue or fight.

This definition differs slightly from the definition presented by Olweus (1997):

> We say a student is being bullied when another student, or a group of students, say nasty and unpleasant things to him or her. It is also bullying when a student is hit, kicked, threatened, locked inside a room, and things like that. These things may take place frequently

and it is difficult for the student being bullied to defend himself or herself. It is also bullying when a student is teased repeatedly in a negative way. But it is not bullying when two students of about the same strength quarrel or fight.

We modified the original Olweus definition slightly in hopes of making the phrasing more congruent with the language of our student population. The Olweus definition of bullying has been revised in recent years (Solberg & Olweus, 2003), but in general calls the student's attention to verbal and physical forms of bullying, and distinguishes between bullying and a conflict between students of comparable strength or status. The revised Olweus definition of bullying also includes social forms of bullying such as excluding someone from a group of friends or attempting to make others dislike someone (Solberg & Olweus, 2003), an area included in the definition used in the present study.

Following the definition of bullying, students were asked to report the number of times in the past month that they have been bullied using this definition ("By this definition, I have been bullied in the past month"). They were also asked about the number of times they bullied others in the past month ("By this definition, I have bullied others in the past month"). Response alternatives were "never," "once or twice," "about once per week," and "several times per week."

The peer nomination instrument presented students and teachers with the same definition of bullying used on the *School Climate Survey* and asked them to respond to two items: "List three students in your classroom who are bullied often," and "List three students in your classroom who frequently bully others." Students did not identify themselves on this form, so that their answers were anonymous.

We collected data on school discipline problems from school records. Teachers routinely completed discipline referral forms for any of 52 possible behavior problems. We identified 17 types of school discipline referrals generally associated with physical or verbal aggression, including bullying, bus discipline, discrimination, disruptive behavior, fighting/no major injury, fighting/major injury, harassment, inappropriate touch, physical assault, sexual assault, sexual harassment, threaten staff, threaten student, uncooperative, possession of a weapon/non-firearm, and possession of a weapon/firearm. Although initially we hoped to focus on referrals for bullying, we learned that teachers rarely used this category and instead preferred to use a category such as "disruptive behavior" or "threaten student" even if they suspected that bullying was taking place. In addition, we were advised that teachers differed in the categories they might choose to describe the same misbehavior. Therefore, we summed the number of discipline referrals across categories. We also tabulated the number of times that a student received after-school detention or was suspended from school. We expected that these three discipline measures would be overlapping and therefore highly correlated with one another, but because they represent indices of successively more serious problem behavior, we decided to investigate all three. We found that office referrals and detentions were correlated .90 (Pearson *r*), office referrals and suspensions were correlated .80, and detentions and suspensions were correlated .62 (all $p < .001$).

Procedure

The survey was administered in classrooms approximately one month following the start of school. Surveys were administered school wide on the same day (although 36 students who were absent on the first day completed the survey on a later date). Teachers using a standard set of directions administered surveys. Students were asked to read the survey carefully and to answer questions honestly. Students were assured that their responses would be used only for research purposes. Students were told not to write their name on the survey itself, but to complete the survey and seal it into an envelope with their name printed on the outside. Each student was assigned a code number, and this number was used to link the two administrations of the survey. Researchers were available in each classroom to answer teacher or student questions. Students who were not participating in the study were asked to sit quietly and work on their school assignments.

A week following survey administration, students and teachers completed the student nomination measures. The student nominations were conducted by the middle school independently of the research project, as part of a school-wide effort by the school counselors to identify victims of bullying. Therefore, all students in the school participated in the nomination procedure, but only results for the students with research consent were included in this study.

RESULTS

Bully Victims

On the self-report survey, two-thirds (66.8%, 278) of the students reported no experiences of being bullied in the past month, one-quarter (25.7%, 107) reported being bullied "once or twice," 4.1% (17) reported being bullied "about once per week," and 3.4% (14) reported being bullied "several times per week." We combined the last two response categories to designate 7.5% of students as victims of bullying. This frequency of being bullied–once per week or more–most closely corresponded to the frequency of "2 or 3 times a month" recommended by Solberg and Olweus (2003).

Agreement with Teacher and Peer Nominations. Our first set of analyses concerned the agreement among student self-report, peer nomination, and teacher nomination of students as victims of bullying. As reported in Table 1, of the 416 student participants, 248 (59.6%) received no peer nominations as victims, 76 (18.3%) received one nomination, 35 (8.4%) received two nominations, and 57 (13.7%) received three or more nominations. Strikingly, four students received more than 20 nominations by their classmates and one student received 65 nominations. The Pearson correlation between student self-report and peer nomination was .17, $p < .001$.

Next, we compared those students who were nominated by at least one classmate with student self-report of being bullied at least once or more per week. This 2×2 table comparison (see Table 1 lower section) yielded 12 students who were identified as victims by both measures, 19 who were identified as victims by self-report but not peers, 156 who were identified by peers but not self-report, and 229 who were identified by neither self-report or peers. The percent agreement between self and peer report was 57.9%, with a kappa coefficient of $-.006$, ns.

We recognized that it might not be considered suitable to identify a student as a victim of bullying based on the report of a single peer, and so we examined other possible cutoffs. When the cutoff for victim status was set at two student nominations, the kappa value was only .02, ns, and for three student nominations the kappa value was .04, ns. The cell frequencies for all 2×2 tables used in determining these kappa values are presented in the lower section of Table 1.

As a final assessment of the correspondence between peer nominations and self-report, we conducted a Receiver Operating Characteristic (ROC) analysis to evaluate the correspondence between the two measures at all possible cutoff scores (Mossman, 1994). An ROC analysis plots the sensitivity and 1-specificity values associated with all possible cutoff scores on a test (in this case, peer nominations) to identify a specified condition (in this case, self-reported victim status). The area under the curve (AUC) in the ROC plot indicates the test's diagnostic efficiency and approximates the common language effect size. A value of .50 indicates that the test predicts the condition at a chance level, and

TABLE 1. Self-Report and Peer Report of Bully Victimization

Number of peer nominations	Self-report of being bullied in the past month				
	Never	Once or twice	About once per week	Several times per week	Total
0	177	52	8	11	248
1	50	22	4	0	76
2	22	11	1	1	35
3	14	5	0	1	20
4	1	5	1	0	7
5	3	4	1	0	8
6	2	0	0	0	2
7	2	4	0	0	6
8	1	0	0	0	1
9	0	0	1	0	1
10	2	1	0	0	3
11	1	0	0	0	1
12	1	0	0	0	1
13	0	0	1	0	1
16 to 65	2	3	0	1	6
Total	278	107	17	14	416

Cutoff points	No more than once or twice "Non-victim"	Once per week or more "Victim"	Total
0	229	19	248
1 to 65	156	12	168
0 to 1	301	23	324
2 to 65	84	8	92
0 to 2	334	25	359
3 to 65	51	6	57

values greater than .50 indicate improvement over chance prediction. For the prediction of victim status using peer nominations, the AUC was .509. The highest obtained sensitivity was .39 with a cutoff of 1 or more peer nominations indicating victim status, and with this cutoff, specificity was .60.

Next, we examined the correspondence between student self-report and teacher nominations. Because teachers only nominated students in their own classes, students were classified as victims if they were identified as a victim by a single teacher. By this measure, 26 (6.3%) students were identified as victims (see Table 2). The Pearson correlation between student self-report (using all four response categories) and teacher nomination was .12, $p < .05$. We then compared those students identified as victims by teachers with student self-report of being bullied at least once or more per week. This comparison yielded just 3 students who were identified as victims by both measures, 28 who were identified as victims by self-report but not teachers, 23 who were identified by teachers but not self-report, and 362 who were identified by neither self-report nor teachers. The percent agreement between self- and teacher report was 87.7%, but the kappa coefficient was .04, ns.

The third and final comparison was between teacher and peer nomination. The Pearson correlation between teacher and peer nomination was .28, $p < .001$. A comparison of those students who were nominated by at least one classmate with those nominated by teachers yielded 22 students who were identified as victims by both measures, 4 who were identified as victims by teachers but not peers, 146 who were identified by peers but not teachers, and 244 who were identified by neither teachers nor peers. The percent agreement between teacher and peer report was 63.9%, with a kappa coefficient of .13, $p < .001$. When the cutoff for victim status was set at two student nominations, the kappa value rose to .29, $p < .001$, and for three student nominations the kappa value was .30, $p < .001$. The cell frequencies for these calculations can be found in Table 3.

An ROC analysis using peer nominations to predict teacher nomination status yielded an AUC of .83. The highest obtained sensitivity was .85 with a cutoff of 1 or more peer nominations indicating victim status, but with this cutoff specificity was .63. When the cutoff was set at

TABLE 2. Self-Report and Teacher Report of Bully Victimization

Teacher nomination as a victim	Self-report of being bullied in the past month				
	Never	Once or twice	About once per week	Several times per week	Total
No	258	98	14	12	382
Yes	20	9	3	2	34
Total	278	107	17	14	416
	No more than once or twice "Non-victim"		Once per week or more "Victim"		
No	362		28		390
Yes	23		3		26
Total	385		31		416

TABLE 3. Teacher Report and Peer Report of Bully Victimization

Number of peer nominations	Teacher identification of student as a victim of bullying		
	Not identified	Identified victim	Total
0	244	4	248
1	75	1	76
2	29	6	35
3	18	2	20
4	5	2	7
5	5	3	8
6	1	1	2
7	4	2	6
8	0	1	1
9	1	0	1
10	3	0	3
11	0	1	1
12	1	1	1
13	0	0	1
16 to 65	4	2	6
Total	390	26	416
Cutoff points			
0	244	4	248
1 to 65	146	22	168
0 to 1	319	5	324
2 to 65	71	21	92
0 to 2	348	11	359
3 to 65	42	15	57

2 or more peer nominations, the sensitivity dropped only slightly to .81, but specificity improved to .82. This appeared to be the optimal cut point.

Prediction of School Discipline Outcomes. The three measures of victim status were correlated with the number of times a student was referred to the principal's office for a discipline problem, number of after-school detentions, and number of suspensions from school. As reported in Table 4, the only statistically significant correlations were between teacher victim status and discipline referrals, .148, $p < .01$, and between teacher victim status and school detentions, .155, $p < .01$.

TABLE 4. Correlations Between Victim Status and School Discipline Infractions

School discipline measure	Self-report as victim	Peer report as victim	Teacher report as victim
Office referral	.025	.029	.148**
Detention	.037	.048	.155**
Suspension	−.008	−.025	.016

Note. ** $p < .01$

We wondered if the correlation between victim status and discipline problems might be due to the presence of students who were victims and bullies, so-called bully-victims (Brockenbrough, Cornell, & Loper, 2002; Olweus, 1993). We inspected the data and found that, among the students identified as victims by teachers, there were three students also identified as bullies by teachers, six students identified as bullies by two or more peers (including one also identified by teachers), and one student who self-identified as bully. Altogether, there were nine students identified as victims by teachers who were also identified as a bully by teacher, peer, or self-report measures. After omitting these nine cases, the correlations between teacher victim status and discipline referrals ($r = .073$) and teacher victim status and school detentions ($r = .067$) were no longer statistically significant.

Bullies

Few students reported bullying others on the self-report survey. Nearly three-quarters (74.8%, 311) denied ever bullying another student in the past month, whereas 21.6% (90) reported bullying just "once or twice." Only 1.4% (6 students) reported bullying others "about once per week" and 2.2% (9 students) reported bullying others "several times per week." Again, we combined the highest two frequencies to designate 3.6% of students as bullies.

Agreement with Teacher and Peer Nominations. We next compared student self-report with peer and teacher nomination of students as bullies. As reported in Table 5, of the 416 student participants, 277 (64%) received no nominations as bullies, 60 (14%) received one nomination, 22 (5%) received two nominations, and the remaining 57 (14%) received three or more nominations. Eight students received 10 or more nominations by their classmates. The Pearson correlation between student self-report and peer nomination was .10, $p < .05$.

TABLE 5. Self-Report and Peer Report of Bullying

Number of peer nominations	Self-report of bullying others in the past month				
	Never	Once or twice	About once per week	Several times per week	Total
0	214	53	5	5	277
1	39	20	1	0	60
2	15	6	0	1	22
3	18	3	0	0	21
4	3	0	0	0	3
5	8	2	0	0	10
6	5	2	0	0	7
7	3	2	0	1	6
9	1	1	0	0	2
11	0	1	0	0	1
12	2	0	0	0	2
13	0	0	0	2	2
15	1	0	0	0	1
16	1	0	0	0	1
22	1	0	0	0	1
Total	311	90	6	9	416

Cutoff points	No more than once or twice "Non-victim"	Once per week or more "Victim"	
0	267	10	277
1 to 65	134	5	139
0 to 1	326	11	337
2 to 65	75	4	79
0 to 2	347	12	359
3 to 65	54	3	57

Next, we compared those students who were nominated by at least one classmate with student self-report of bullying at least once or more per week. This comparison yielded just 5 students who were identified as bullies by both measures, 10 who were identified as bullies by self-report but not peers, 134 who were identified by peers but not self-report, and 267 who were identified by neither self-report nor peers. The percent agreement between self- and peer report was 65%, but the kappa coefficient was .00, p = ns.

Again because it might not be considered suitable to identify a student as a bully based on the report of a single peer, we examined other possible cutoffs. If the cutoff for bully status was set at two student nominations, the kappa value was .026, p = ns, and for three student nominations the kappa value was .028, p = ns. The cell frequencies for these calculations are in Table 5.

As a final assessment of the correspondence between peer nominations and self-reported bullying, we conducted a Receiver Operating Characteristic (ROC) analysis to evaluate the correspondence between the two measures at all possible cutoff scores (Mossman, 1994). For the prediction of bully status using peer nominations, the AUC was .52. The highest obtained sensitivity was .33 with a cutoff of 1 or more peer nominations indicating bully status, and with this cutoff, specificity was .67.

Next, we examined the correspondence between student self-report and teacher identification of the student as a bully. By the teacher identification measure, 34 (8%) students were identified as bullies (see Table 6). The Pearson correlation between student self-report (using all four response categories) and teacher nomination was .05, p = ns. We then compared those students identified as bullies by teachers with student self-report of bullying others at least once or more per week. This 2 × 2 table comparison yielded only two students who were identified as bullies by both measures, 13 who were identified as bullies by self-report but not teachers, 32 who were identified by teachers but not self-report, and 369 who were identified by neither self-report nor teachers. The percent agreement between self- and teacher report was 89%, with a kappa coefficient of .03, p = ns.

TABLE 6. Self-Report and Teacher Report of Bullying

Teacher nomination as a bully	Self-report of bullying others in the past month				
	Never	Once or twice	About once per week	Several times per week	Total
No	287	82	6	7	382
Yes	24	8	0	2	34
Total	311	90	6	9	416
	No more than once or twice "Non-bully"		Once per week or more "Bully"		
No	369		13		382
Yes	32		2		34
Total	401		15		416

The third and final comparison was between teacher and peer nomination. The Pearson correlation between teacher and peer nomination was .52, $p < .001$. A comparison of those students who were nominated by at least one classmate with those nominated by teachers yielded 30 students who were identified as bullies by both measures, 4 who were identified as bullies by teachers but not peers, 109 who were identified by peers but not teachers, and 273 who were identified by neither teachers nor peers. The percent agreement between teacher and peer report was 73%, with a kappa coefficient of .25, $p < .001$. If the cutoff for bully status was set at two peer nominations, the kappa value was .37, $p < .001$, and for three student nominations the kappa value was .40, $p < .001$. The cell frequencies for these calculations are reported in Table 7. An ROC analysis using peer nominations to predict teacher nomination status yielded an AUC of .86. The highest obtained sensitivity was .88 with a cutoff of 1 or more peer nominations indicating victim status, and with this cutoff, specificity was .72.

Prediction of School Discipline Outcomes. As reported in Table 8, there were statistically significant correlations between self-reported bullying and subsequent school discipline referrals ($r = .121$, $p < .05$, and school suspensions ($r = .099$, $p < .05$). Peer nominations of bullying were correlated with subsequent school discipline referrals ($r = .410$, $p < .001$), detentions ($r = .339$, $p < .001$), and suspensions ($r = .393$, $p < .001$). Teacher nominations of bullying were correlated with subsequent school discipline referrals ($r = .385$, $p < .001$), detentions ($r = .341$, $p < .001$), and suspensions ($r = .359$, $p < .001$). We compared the magnitude of the three correlations for self-report with the corresponding correlations for peer and teacher nominations using r-to-z transformation. All six of the correlations for peers and teacher nominations were significantly larger ($p < .01$) than the corresponding correlations using self-report data.

DISCUSSION

Our findings raise concern about reliance solely on student self-report to identify bullies and victims of bullying. Students were given a common definition of bullying and asked to identify the frequency of their involvement in bullying others or being bullied in the past month. Overall, there was poor correspondence between self-reported involvement in bullying–as victim or perpetrator–and either peer or teacher nomination measures.

TABLE 7. Teacher Report and Peer Report of Bullying

Number of peer nominations	Teacher identification of student as a victim of bullying		
	Not identified	Identified victim	Total
0	273	4	277
1	55	5	60
2	18	4	22
3	18	3	21
4	2	1	3
5	5	5	10
6	5	2	7
7	4	2	6
9	1	1	2
11	0	1	1
12	0	2	2
13	0	2	2
15 to 22	1	2	3
Total	382	34	416
Cutoff points			
0	273	4	277
1 to 65	109	30	139
0 to 1	328	9	337
2 to 65	54	25	79
0 to 2	346	13	359
3 to 65	36	21	57

TABLE 8. Correlations Between Bully Status and School Discipline Measures

School discipline measure	(1) Self-report as bully	(2) Peer report as bully	(3) Teacher report as bully	(1) vs (2) z value	(1) vs (3) z value
Office referral	.121*	.410***	.385***	6.40**	5.79**
Detention	.074	.339***	.341***	5.69**	5.69**
Suspension	.099*	.393***	.359***	6.34**	5.63**

Note. * $p < .05$; ** $p < .01$; *** $p < .001$. $N = 416$. Correlations in column (1) compared to correlations in columns (2) and (3) using Fisher r-to-z transformation.

For self-reported involvement as a victim of bullying, we could find only a weak correlation ($r = .17$) between self-report and peer report. All of the kappa coefficients used to measure the correspondence between self-report and peer report as dichotomous indicators of bullying (victim or non-victim) were statistically nonsignificant. Using Receiver Operating Characteristic analysis, we found an AUC of just .509, which represents virtually no improvement over chance (.50), in the identification of self-reported victims using peer reports as a predictor. These findings are particularly discouraging in light of other work on the concordance between self- and peer reports of victimization, which generally report statistically significant correlations, some as high as .50. However, these measurements typically are based on multi-item scales, and participants may receive training before they make self- or peer ratings (for example, see Ladd & Kochenderfer-Ladd, 2002).

One particularly troubling observation was that there were students who were clearly identified as victims of bullying by their peers yet did not report themselves as victims of bullying. For example, of the 12 students who were identified as victims of bullying by 10 or more classmates, 6 denied ever being bullied in the past month and 4 reported being bullied just "once or twice." Only two students would have been identified as victims of bullying by the criterion that the student reported being bullied at least once a week. This raises the possibility that students may underreport their victim experiences, perhaps because of denial, embarrassment, or shame.

We also observed potential overreporting of student victimization experiences. There were 11 students who claimed to be victims of bullying several times per week, and 8 who claimed to be victims about once per week, who nevertheless were not identified by any of their classmates as victims of bullying. If these student self-reports are accurate, then these observations indicate a limitation in peer nominations as an indicator of victims of bullying, but without an independent criterion it is not possible to determine which measure is more accurate. These conflicting observations underscore the need for more extensive study of current methods of identifying victims of bullying.

Teacher identification of bullies also showed little correspondence with student self-report. The Pearson correlation between teacher and self-report was just .12, and the kappa coefficient for the correspondence between teacher and self-report was statistically nonsignificant. However, it is reasonable to question whether the low correspondence between self- and teacher ratings could be due in part to limitations in teacher awareness of bullying. Of the 31 students who reported they were victims of bullying at least once per week, teachers identified only 3. Craig, Pepler, and Atlas (2000) found that teachers may often overlook bullying, and similarly, a study of middle school students by Unnever and Cornell (2003b) found that students believe teachers frequently fail to act in response to bullying.

We found limited correspondence between student self-report of bullying and peer nomination. The correlation between self- and peer reports of bullying was just .10. The kappa coefficients for the correspondence between self-report and peer nomination of bullying were all nonsignificant. The AUC from the ROC analysis was just .52, indicating virtually no improvement over chance in the identification of self-reported bullies using peer nominations.

We found that relatively few students identified themselves as bullies on the self-report survey. Only 15 students admitted bullying others at least once per week, a prevalence rate of just 3.6%. This prevalence level compares to 6.5% reported by Solberg and Olweus (2003) for a Norwegian sample of students in grades 5-9 and 9.8% to 10.4% for students in grades 6-8 in a U.S. national sample (Nansel et al., 2001). Although an additional 90 students were willing to admit bullying classmates once or twice in the past month, this frequency is usually not regarded as sufficient to identify a student as a bully (Solberg & Olweus, 2003). The relatively low rate of self-reported bullying in our sample could be attributable to differences in survey wording, including the definition of bullying and the response categories presented to students, in comparison to surveys used in other studies. If so, this conclusion would argue for more careful attention to survey development and standardization. Currently there are a wide range of definitions and formats for surveying students about bullying.

Another possibility is that students were less willing to admit bullying on our survey because their answers were not anonymous. Students were assured of confidentiality, and they were told that their answers would be used only for research purposes and not disclosed to school personnel, but it is conceivable that some students nevertheless were reluctant to admit bullying others. To our knowledge, differences in student reporting to anonymous versus confidential surveys have not been investigated, but clearly should be studied. If students respond in a markedly different way to confidential surveys that are not anonymous, it would pose a substantial barrier to cross-informant or multi-method research on bullying. Studies that rely on anonymous self-report are limited in value because student report cannot be compared to other sources of information and student responses cannot be studied within a more powerful longitudinal framework.

The modest level of self-reported bullying in this study contrasts markedly with peer nominations. Students identified 149 classmates as bullies, which is nearly 36% of the sample and 10 times the self-reported rate. If the definition of bullying is limited to those identified by at least three classmates, the number of bullies drops to 69, or about 17% of the sample.

There was an absence of correspondence between teacher identification of bullies and student self-report. Both the Pearson correlation and the kappa coefficient for correspondence between teacher and self-report were not statistically significant. Teachers named only 2 of the 15 students who identified themselves as bullies. Again, this finding may be consistent with student perceptions that teachers are not sensitive to or aware of bullying that occurs (Unnever & Cornell, 2003b).

Correspondence Between Peer and Teacher Nominations

Although there was poor agreement between student self-report and either peer or teacher nominations, the two nomination measures showed more consistent correspondence, perhaps in part due to shared method variance. For the identification of victims of bullying, teacher and peer nominations correlated .28, and the ROC analysis generated a substantial AUC effect size of .83. Kappa coefficients for the correspondence between teacher identification and one, two, or three peer nominations as a victim were .13, .29, and .30, respectively, all statistically significant, $p < .001$. Using a cutoff of two peer nominations generated the most accurate predictions of teacher nominations, with a sensitivity of .81 and specificity of .82. In contrast, Nabuzoka (2003) found a statistically nonsignificant correlation (Spearman's rho) of just .15 between peer and teacher ratings with a sample of 55 children (ages 8-12) and their teachers.

For the identification of bullies, peer and teacher nominations showed similarly impressive agreement. The Pearson correlation between peer and teacher nominations was .52. This result compares favorably to the Spearman rho correlation of .45 found by Nabuzoka (2003) in a study of peer and teacher ratings for 55 school children. Using cutoffs for bully status of one, two, or three peer nominations generated kappa coefficients of .25, .37, and .40, respectively, all statistically significant, $p < .001$. The ROC analysis yielded an effect size of .86. A cutoff of one peer nomination generated the most accurate predictions of teacher nominations, with a sensitivity of .88 and specificity of .72.

The relatively good cross-informant agreement between peers and teachers raises the credibility of each measure and casts further doubt on the accuracy of student self-report. In contrast, Solberg and Olweus (2003) criticized the use of peer nominations in favor of student self-report for a variety of reasons. They pointed out the arbitrariness of determining a cutoff point for the number of nominations needed to indicate a student has been bullied or has been a bully, and contended that further arbitrary differences might arise because classrooms vary in the number of students making ratings. They also pointed out that peer nominations might yield different results based on how the questions are posed to students and how many students they are asked to nominate. However, all of these objections might be overcome with standardization derived from systematic research. Moreover, similar shortcomings and arbitrariness can be observed with student self-report. Although the cutoff in peer nominations needed to identify a student as a victim or bully can seem arbitrary, so too on self-report surveys the frequency necessary to designate a student as victim or bully (once a week, more than once a week, etc.) can seem arbitrary. Solberg and Olweus (2003) conducted a study to determine the most useful cut points for self-report surveys, and similar research can be conducted for peer nominations.

Prediction of Student Discipline Problems

As expected, students identified as bullies subsequently were more likely than other students to receive school discipline referrals, and in the more serious cases, receive consequences such as after-school detentions and suspensions from school. Notably, the correlations with peer nominations (range .34 to .41) and teacher nominations (range .34 to .39) were all significantly larger ($p < .01$) than the corresponding correlations obtained with self-reports (range .07 to .12). This observation is consistent with the contention that peer and teacher identification of bullies has greater validity than identification by self-report, or at least that those bullies identified by peers and teachers are more likely to be students who commit school discipline infractions. To some extent, the correspondence between teacher identification of bullies and school discipline referrals could reflect mere consistency, as distinguished from validity, of teacher perceptions of their students. In other words, teachers who perceive a student to be a bully may be more inclined to make a discipline referral.

Although school discipline records are not a sufficient indicator of bullying to establish differential validity for self-, peer, and teacher measures, nevertheless, they do support the need for comparative research. Such research might involve more direct assessment of student bullying through interview and observational methods to provide a more definitive criterion of bullying, or perhaps outcome research could determine which indicators are most sensitive to intervention. We recognize that many acts of bullying, particularly social or relational bullying, may not rise to the level of a school discipline infraction.

We did not expect to find high levels of discipline infractions among victims of bullying, although in retrospect some studies have identified a subgroup of victims who also engage in bullying or related aggressive behavior (Brockenbrough, 2001; Brockenbrough et al., 2002; Haynie et al., 2001). Interestingly, the only statistically significant correlations were obtained with teacher nominations. This might imply that teachers are most aware of those victims of bullying who are prone to misbehavior, perhaps because these students bring more attention to themselves. When we omitted the teacher-identified victims who were also identified as bullies (by teachers, peers, or self-report), the correlations between victim status and the three school discipline measures were no longer statistically significant.

Other Study Limitations

This study does not demonstrate that all forms of student self-report are problematic or that student self-report cannot be used to identify bullies or victims of bullying. We used a definition modeled after the Olweus definition (Olweus, 1997), but did not test the more recent, revised version (Solbert & Olweus, 2003). The accuracy of student self-report might be improved with a better definition of bullying or the use of a series of questions about bullying. It also might be possible to improve student self-reporting with classroom instruction on bullying so that students had a clearer understanding of bullying before they completed the survey. Also, we have not examined in this study the potential value of validity check items ("I am telling the truth on this survey") or other screening techniques to eliminate invalid surveys (Cornell & Loper, 1998). At this stage, we know too little about the conditions under which student self-report can be used as a reliable and valid measure of student involvement in bullying.

Although the student self-report and peer nomination measures presented students with the same definition of bullying, there were some differences in the procedures that could have contributed to the low correspondence between them. The self-report survey asked students to rate the frequency of being bullied or bullying others in the past month, whereas the peer nomination form asked students to identify classmates to who are bullied "often" and classmates who "frequently bully others." In addition, the peer nomination procedure invited students to nominate up to three classmates, which may have helped increase the number of students reported as victims or bullies relative to the self-report.

We compared student self-report to peer and teacher nominations, but peer and teacher nominations are not entirely accurate indicators of student involvement in bullying either. Peers may nominate classmates for a variety of reasons, and in some cases nominate students because their behavior has seemed inappropriate or deserving of criticism (Teraesahjo & Salmivalli, 2003). A single peer nomination may not be sufficient to indicate bullying, and researchers may want to use multiple-item scales or ratings to identify bullies and victims, similar to research on peer aggression (Ladd & Kochenderfer-Ladd, 2002).

Teachers may not be sufficiently aware of the nature and extent of bullying among their students. Craig et al. (2000) conducted an observational study of bullying in playground and classroom settings. They found that peers were present as observers during most bullying episodes regardless of the setting. However, teachers seldom intervened to stop bullying, either because they failed to recognize what was going on or perhaps because they chose to ignore it.

Clearly, further research investigating multiple forms of bully and victim identification is needed. Repeated observation and interviewing of students might be one approach to assess the full extent of bullying in a school or classroom, and might provide a firmer basis for comparisons with less labor intensive and more efficient methods such as student surveys.

Study Implications

The purpose of this study is not to reject the use of student self-report in favor of nomination procedures, but to point out the lack of correspondence between these two commonly used methods and to argue for more careful investigation of the measurement properties of both instruments. Student self-report is the predominant method used in bullying research today, and pervades more general research on aggressive and high-risk behavior in schools (Cornell & Loper, 1998), yet the reliability and validity of many student self-report measures are not well established. We have made good use of student self-report in previous studies

(Cornell & Loper, 1998; Unnever & Cornell, 2003a, 2003b), but believe that independent verification of student bully and victim status would enhance the credibility, and likely strengthen the findings, of such studies.

We need to determine the most appropriate wording for questions about bullying behavior, or at least the impact of wording differences on student responses, as well as the effect of different procedures and administration conditions on survey results. Such research may not seem attractive to researchers because it is methodological and technical, but it is essential to the development of instruments that can be used in substantive research and theory testing. Even if the differences among student, peer, and teacher perceptions in this study were found to be entirely artifacts of subtle differences in measurement procedures (such as the wording of questions), the fact that these differences in procedure could have such impact on results must be recognized.

We are particularly concerned about the reliance on student self-report in studies of bullying interventions (Olweus et al., 1998). Self-report surveys are attractive because they represent such an economical and efficient way to gather a large amount of quantitative data, and schools are willing to tolerate the relatively brief disruption they cause in the school day. Although some researchers using student self-reports have found statistically significant reductions in bullying behavior with their interventions, the magnitude of change is quite varied, and in some studies the results seem small relative to the extent of the school intervention (Brockenbrough, 2001; Olweus et al., 1998; Smith, 1997). If student self-report does not accurately measure the prevalence of student bullying, then it will not be possible to assess accurately the effectiveness of school interventions, and a small or statistically insignificant magnitude of change could be an artifact of measurement error rather than intervention weakness. In summarizing results of the Sheffield Anti-Bullying project involving 23 United Kingdom schools, Smith (1997) reported that some schools found small reductions in bullying according to self-reports of being bullied and bullying others, but more substantial improvement on other indicators of change, such as student-initiated contacts with teachers to stop bullying and the proportion of bullied students who said someone talked to them about it. Perhaps student self-report of bullying was not adequately sensitive to the change taking place in these schools. In conclusion, we recommend that studies of bullying interventions rely on multiple measures, including student self-report and informant nominations, as a well as review of school discipline referrals, in order to gather a more comprehensive assessment of intervention outcomes.

NOTE

1. It is also desirable to examine the internal consistency of survey responses, to include validity check items ("I am telling the truth on this survey"), and to inspect surveys for extreme response patterns, but such procedures do not appear to be widely used in bullying research or school survey research in general (see Cornell & Loper, 1998). Use of internal check procedures would improve the routine use of student surveys, but would not eliminate the need for validational research using external criteria.

REFERENCES

Achenbach, T. M., McConaughy, S. H., & Howell, C. T. (1987). Child/adolescent behavioral and emotional problems: Implications of cross-informant correlations for situational specificity. *Psychological Bulletin, 101,* 213-232.

Brockenbrough, K. (2001). *Peer victimization and bullying prevention among middle school students.* Unpublished doctoral dissertation, Curry School of Education, University of Virginia.

Brockenbrough, K., Cornell, D. G., & Loper, A. B. (2002). Aggressive victims of violence at school. *Education and Treatment of Children, 25,* 273-287.

Cornell, D. G., & Loper, A. B. (1998). Assessment of violence and other high-risk behaviors with a school survey. *School Psychology Review, 27,* 317-330.

Craig, W. M., Pepler, D., & Atlas, R. (2000). Observations of bullying in the playground and in the classroom. *School Psychology International, 21,* 22-36.

Haynie, D. L., Nansel, T., Eitel, P., Crump, A. D., Saylor, K., Yu, K., & Simons-Morton, B. (2001). Bullies, victims, and bully/victims: Distinct groups of at-risk youth. *Journal of Early Adolescence, 21,* 29-49.

Ladd, G. W., & Kochenderfer-Ladd, B. (2002). Identifying victims of peer aggression from early to middle childhood: Analysis of cross-informant data for concordance, estimation of relational adjustment, prevalence of victimization, and characteristics of identified victims. *Psychological Assessment, 14,* 74-96.

Mossman, D. (1994). Assessing predictions of violence: Being accurate about accuracy. *Journal of Consulting and Clinical Psychology, 62,* 783-792.

Nabuzoka, D. (2003). Teacher ratings and peer nominations of bullying and other behaviour of children with and without learning difficulties. *Educational Psychology, 23,* 307-321.

Nansel, T. R., Overpeck, M., Pilla, R. S., Ruan, W. J., Simons-Morton, B., & Scheidt, P. (2001). Bullying behaviors among U.S. youth, prevalence and association with psychosocial adjustment. *The Journal of the American Medical Association, 285,* 2094-2100.

Olweus, D. (1993). *Bullying at school: What we know and what we can do.* Oxford, GB: Blackwell.

Olweus, D. (1997). Bully/victim problems in school: Knowledge base and an effective intervention program. *The Irish Journal of Psychology, 18,* 170-190.

Olweus, D., Limber, S., & Mihalic, S. F. (1998). *Bullying prevention program.* In D. S. Elliott (Series Ed.), *Blueprints for violence prevention.* Boulder, CO: Center for the

Study and Prevention of Violence, Institute of Behavioral Science, University of Colorado at Boulder.

Perry, D. G., Kusel, S. J., & Perry, L. C. (1988). Victims of peer aggression. *Developmental Psychology, 24*, 807-814.

Smith, P. K. (1997). Bullying in schools: The UK experience and the Sheffield Anti-Bullying project. *The Irish Journal of Psychology, 18*, 191-201.

Solberg, M. E., & Olweus, D. (2003). Prevalence estimation of school bullying with the Olweus Bully/Victim Questionnaire. *Aggressive Behavior, 29*, 239-268.

Teraesahjo, T., & Salmivalli, C. (2003). "She is not actually bullied." The discourse of harassment in student groups. *Aggressive Behavior, 29*, 134-154.

Unnever, J., & Cornell, D. G. (2003a). Bullying, self-control, and ADHD. *Journal of Interpersonal Violence, 18*, 129-147.

Unnever, J., & Cornell, D. G. (2003b). The culture of bullying in middle school. *Journal of School Violence, 2*, 5-28.

Data Quality in Student Risk Behavior Surveys and Administrator Training

Jennifer E. Cross
Rebecca Newman-Gonchar

SUMMARY. This study examined the influence of survey validity screening on the results from three group-administered school surveys administered to samples totaling approximately 5500 students in 19 schools. The estimated levels of risk behaviors, antisocial behaviors, and victim experiences were substantially reduced when respondents who gave multiple inconsistent or extreme responses to other survey items were screened out of the data. The researchers also observed that the percentage of students giving inconsistent and illogically extreme responses was greater among those surveys given by an untrained administrator, raising the hypothesis that administrator training could be a critical fac-

Jennifer E. Cross is a research associate with the Research and Development Center for the Advancement of Student Learning and Assistant Professor in the Department of Sociology at Colorado State University.

Rebecca Newman-Gonchar is a doctoral student in the School of Education at Colorado State University.

Address correspondence to: Jennifer Cross, Department of Sociology, B258 Andrew G. Clark Building, Colorado State University, Fort Collins, CO 80523-1784 (E-mail: jecross@lamar.colostate.edu).

This research was conducted as part of the local evaluation of a Safe Schools/ Healthy Students Initiative. The authors would like to thank the many teachers and administrators who helped in the collection of data for this research. They also thank their colleague, Michael Lacy, for his assistance and critical insight; Erin Grummert for her assistance; and the reviewers for their enormously helpful constructive criticism.

[Haworth co-indexing entry note]: "Data Quality in Student Risk Behavior Surveys and Administrator Training." Cross, Jennifer E.. and Rebecca Newman-Gonchar. Co-published simultaneously in *Journal of School Violence* (The Haworth Press, Inc.) Vol. 3, No. 2/3, 2004, pp. 89-108; and: *Issues in School Violence Research* (ed: Michael J. Furlong et al.) The Haworth Press, Inc., 2004, pp. 89-108. Single or multiple copies of this article are available for a fee from The Haworth Document Delivery Service [1-800-HAWORTH, 9:00 a.m. - 5:00 p.m. (EST). E-mail address: docdelivery@haworthpress.com].

http://www.haworthpress.com/web/JSV
© 2004 by The Haworth Press, Inc. All rights reserved.
Digital Object Identifier: 10.1300/J202v03n02_06

tor in obtaining more consistent and trustworthy survey data. These results indicate that it may be important to train school staff in survey
administration and to screen surveys for validity in order to improve the
accuracy of student self-report surveys. *[Article copies available for a fee
from The Haworth Document Delivery Service: 1-800-HAWORTH. E-mail
address: <docdelivery@haworthpress.com> Website: <http://www.HaworthPress.
com> © 2004 by The Haworth Press, Inc. All rights reserved.]*

KEYWORDS. Data quality, school violence, survey methodology, risk
behaviors

In the past decade, the public has become increasingly concerned
about the safety of students in schools, and the federal government has
dedicated millions of dollars towards the prevention of violence in
schools through the Safe Schools/Healthy Students Initiative and other
programs. As concern for student safety has risen, so has our reliance on
survey data for identifying risks and making policy decisions (Tanur,
1994, p. B1). The most widely reported measures of school violence are
items from self-report surveys administered in schools (Cornell &
Loper, 1998). Results from these surveys are used for a variety of purposes from developing public policy, to identifying problem behaviors
within a particular school or district, to planning and evaluating prevention activities. Yet the data from these surveys are rarely scrutinized for
consistency (Fetters, Stowe, & Owings, 1984).

SCHOOL VIOLENCE SURVEY DATA QUALITY ISSUES
AND CONCERNS

In the field of juvenile delinquency, self-report data have been scrutinized for reliability and validity issues (Elliot, Huizinga, & Menard,
1989). Estimates of juvenile delinquency can vary significantly by data
source, and official records, such as police reports and school incident
reports, typically underreport delinquency (Huizinga & Elliot, 1986).
Delinquent behavior is reported only in these records when juveniles
are caught, which underrepresents the actual frequency of delinquent
behavior. Self-report data may be the closest approximation of actual
delinquency, but they are not free from misrepresentation. Participants
could lie, misunderstand the questions, or forget their previous behav-

iors (Huizinga & Elliot, 1986). "It has become customary . . . for researchers employing self-reported offender data to preface their work with a brief review of research on the reliability and validity of these measures . . ." (p. 323). In some cases, researchers compare the self-report data they have collected with external agency reports, such as police reports (Curry, 2000). In other cases, researchers use test-retest procedures to assure that self-reports remain consistent over time (Brener, Kann, McManus, Kinchen, Sundberg, & Ross, 2002).

Although similar to juvenile delinquency research, school violence research rarely identifies self-report data issues. In fact, recent explorations in the field of school violence prevention have revealed only a few articles identifying reliability and validity research on self-report school violence data (Brener et al., 2002; Cornell & Loper, 1998; Rosenblatt & Furlong, 1997). Survey data should be used with caution because "few surveys undertake rigorous screening for invalid response tendencies or include validity items" (Cornell & Loper, 1998, p. 319), and most research has been published without any reference to reliability and validity checks (Rosenblatt & Furlong, 1997, p. 190).

Rosenblatt and Furlong (1997) used reliability and validity checks to re-analyze data from a larger study of school violence. Those respondents that failed the reliability and validity checks were found to be inconsistent and/or dishonest in their self-reports. Rosenblatt and Furlong compared the responses of students who passed their reliability and validity checks with the responses of students who failed the checks. Those students who failed the reliability and validity checks were the same students who reported dramatically higher rates of violence in their schools. Although only a small percentage of students (1.76%) were labeled as rejected respondents, their reports of violence and victimization inflated the overall rates among the sample. Fifteen percent of rejected respondents reported being a victim of violence at school versus only 2% of the valid respondents (Rosenblatt & Furlong, 1997, p. 197). Unfortunately, as Rosenblatt and Furlong pointed out, data from school violence surveys have been reported and presumed accurate for years without similar checks of reliability and validity.

Cornell and Loper (1998) conducted a similar check of the reliability and validity of a school violence survey. In their study, Cornell and Loper analyzed responses to a School Safety survey and categorized invalid surveys into two groups, inappropriate responses and exaggerated responses. Cornell and Loper found that 24.2% of surveys were found to be invalid. The impact of inconsistent, dishonest, and exaggerated responses on rates of violence and risk behaviors in school was tremendous; exclusion of invalid surveys reduced the reported rate of gun carrying from 16.3% to 5.6% (Cornell & Loper, 1998, p. 322). Reliability and validity checks are needed to accurately report what is happening in schools and what is needed to address problem areas.

Administering surveys in schools to collect data on student perceptions takes advantage of the ready access to large numbers of students, the availability of teachers to administer surveys to a captive audience, and the low cost of large survey distribution (Finkelhor, 1998). However, this approach also has disadvantages that must be acknowledged and examined when reporting data from these surveys. One disadvantage is the reliance on students not only to comprehend the questions being asked (Finkelhor, 1998), but also to provide purposefully true and accurate information (Li, Trivedi, & Guo, 2003). The research in this article suggests an additional disadvantage–survey administrators may impact the students' motivation to provide reliable information, which may increase bias in the results.

Demand effects, the effects of the environment on study subjects, have most often been studied in experimental research (Orne, 1970); however, demand effects also might be examined in the context of survey research. "If subjects have some idea of the purpose of the study or the motivation for doing 'well,' they may alter their behavior to respond more favorably" (Schumacher & McMillan, 1993). Survey respondents may present themselves in a positive or negative light that is not accurate or they may present themselves in the most socially desirable position, answering questions the way they think will be most socially acceptable. Previous research has suggested the tendency of adolescent respondents to exaggerate socially undesirable behaviors–violence and high-risk behaviors (Cornell & Loper, 1998; Rosenblatt & Furlong, 1997).

There are many possible effects that could account for dishonest or exaggerated answers. One effect is the bias of auspices, which suggests that "any change in method of collecting or processing data can be expected to show change in results" (Deming, in Denzin, 1970, p. 328). Bias of auspices purports that knowledge of the survey sponsor may impact the respondents' answers. If the respondents know who is sponsoring the survey, they may change the answers to support or oppose the organization sponsoring the survey.

Little research has been done on how administration conditions and procedures might affect the responses to school-based surveys (Groves, 1987). Research on respondent errors has focused on motivation and social desirability effects, which are linked closely with the rapport between respondents and the survey administrator. "Communicator credibility," or the credibility the survey administrator has with the students, has been shown to affect the participant's desire to do a good job on the survey (Graham, Roberts, Tatterson, & Johnston, 2002). "Thus, anything that enhances the credibility; that is, the perceived expertise and trustworthiness, of the survey session leader should enhance the quality of the data collected" (p. 150). Unfortunately, "large-scale surveys often utilize convenient, cost-effective mechanisms for distribution of questionnaires by giving packets to schools and requesting that teachers administer surveys during a specific class period" (Rosenblatt & Furlong, 1997, p. 199). This procedure for administration does not ensure that each survey administrator has the rapport necessary to encourage honest responses and, therefore, may jeopardize the proportion of valid and consistent responses.

As widely used as group-administered, self-report surveys are, it is interesting to note that few research articles or texts suggest "best practices" for group survey administration. Several researchers point out that this lack of standards is due in part to the fact that survey research "belongs to no particular academic discipline and is governed by none" (Schiltz, 1988, p. 68). While there is a substantial body of literature on public opinion survey methodology (Wiesberg, Krosnick, & Bowen, 1996), less has been written specifically regarding methodological issues for group administered questionnaires. Not only does the lack of commonly referenced standards for survey administration threaten the value of survey results, but the lack of attention to unreliable and invalid responses in published reports also threatens to mislead both the public and policy makers.

AIMS OF THE STUDY

Because decision makers rely on student survey data to inform local and national prevention efforts and policies, it is essential that survey estimates of student involvement in high-risk behaviors are accurate. One great disadvantage of using surveys to collect information on violence and risk behaviors is the susceptibility of survey data to a variety of biases. Most importantly, invalid or exaggerated responses from a small percentage of students can mean significant differences in the interpretation of results. Given these concerns, we examined two questions in this study. First, can unreliable and presumptively invalid responses be easily identified and removed to improve the quality of results? Second, does the training of survey administrators influence the proportion of students who give unreliable and presumptively invalid responses?

METHOD

The data for this study were taken from three surveys administered in a suburban Colorado school district. A different research institute developed each of the three surveys, but all included questions on violence and risk behaviors.

Instruments

The *Colorado Youth Survey (CYS)* was developed by the OMNI Institute of Denver, Colorado. Its questions are based on the Risk and Protective Factor Model developed by the Social Development Research Group at the University of Washington. The version used in this study consisted of 120 questions, some broken into subparts, for a total of 194 items. The survey was eight pages long (four back-to-back sheets), formatted on computer scannable sheets onto which students directly marked their answers. In addition to questions regarding risk and protective factors, the survey also included a variety of outcome questions related to weapons, violence, illegal activities, and substance use.

The *Safe Schools/Healthy Students (SS/HS)* survey was developed by the Research Triangle Institute for the national evaluation of the federal Safe Schools/Healthy Students Initiative. This survey was developed to measure the impact of the initiative on five broad domains: Education Reform; School Safety/Safe School Environment: Alcohol, Tobacco, and Other Drug Use; Violence Prevention; and Mental Health. To address these five areas, the survey included pre-existing questions from a variety of surveys, such as the *Youth Risk Behavior Survey, Monitoring the Future, Social Development Research Group*, and *American Drug and Alcohol Survey*. The survey included 150 questions and was printed in a 16-page booklet. Students marked their answers on a separate computer scannable answer sheet.

The *Perception Survey* was compiled by the Research and Development Center for the Advancement of Student Learning. It was designed to measure student attitudes, behaviors, and perceptions about others' behaviors regarding school climate, violence, and substance use. Questions for this survey were derived from *The Student Norm Survey*, developed by The Alcohol Education Project at Hobart and William Smith Colleges, and from the *Get Real About Violence Survey* developed by the Comprehensive Health Education Foundation. The survey included 45 questions and was printed on four (two back-to-back) pages of paper. Students marked their answers on a separate computer scannable answer sheet.

Participants and Administration

Each of the three surveys was used by a public school district as part of the evaluation of violence and substance abuse prevention programs. The *CYS* was administered to a random sample of classrooms from grades 6, 8, 10, 11, and 12 at 10 schools within the district. The total sample size was 2,295; roughly half (51%) of students were in the 6th through 9th grades, and half (49%) in 10th through 12th grades. Forty-four percent of students left no questions unanswered, and an additional 30% left only one to three items unanswered. This survey was administered to a similar sample of students in the same public school district each March since 1999. Per district policy, students who were not present during the time the survey was administered were not given an opportunity to take the survey at another date. Each year prevention specialists in the district met with school teams to give them written and verbal directions for administering the survey. Working closely with school leaders, the prevention specialists emphasized to the teachers how important presentation of the survey would be to collecting quality data. They directed the teachers to implore the students to be honest and explain how the data would be used by their school to benefit students.

The *SS/HS* was administered to a random sample of classrooms from grades 7, 9, and 11 at the junior highs and high schools not sampled by the *CYS*. The total sample size was 2,720 with two-thirds (67%) of the students in the 7th through 9th grades, and one-third (33%) in 10th through 12th grades. Sixty percent of students left no questions unanswered, and an additional 24% left only one to three items unanswered. This survey was administered on very short notice to schools in November of 2000, and students absent during administration of the survey were not able to complete the survey at another time. Schools were given the choice of having teachers administer the survey or having someone come into the classroom and administer the surveys for them. At those schools where the teachers administered the survey, each teacher was given a packet of surveys with written directions to be read to the students. At those schools where teachers did not administer the surveys, other district personnel read the same written directions. Given the short notice of the survey administration, some teachers did not find out until the day of administration that students in their class would be taking a survey. In comparison to the administration of the *CYS*, training of survey administrators was highly inconsistent.

The *Perception Survey* was administered to 521 10th graders at two high schools in the district. Results from this administration were intended to be used as baseline data for upcoming prevention programming. In the spring of 2002, 192 students at City High School and 243 students at Valley High School took the survey in a required health class. Eighty-seven percent of students taking the survey completed the entire survey and two percent left four or more items unanswered. At Valley High School, prevention specialists who had been brought in to deliver a week of prevention lessons administered the survey on a Monday. At City High School, the prevention specialists had not been invited to deliver the prevention lessons, so the health teachers administered the surveys to their own students. The prevention specialists provided the head of the department with packets of surveys and written directions to be read to the students. The following fall this survey was administered again to 10th-grade health students at City High School. By this time, the prevention specialists had been invited to deliver a week of lessons and they administered the survey on the first day of the week.

Measures of Extremity and Inconsistency

Several survey items were tested to assess the data quality of results from each survey. Twenty-nine items on the *CYS* and 26 similar items on the *SS/HS* were used to identify unreliable (inconsistent) and potentially invalid (illogically extreme) responses. We used slightly fewer questions on the *SS/HS* because that survey had fewer overall questions. On the *Perception Survey*, six questions were used to identify inconsistent and illogically extreme answers. A detailed list of questions and responses used to create the inconsistent and extreme measures is available from the first author.

Respondents that answered inconsistently were considered to be unreliable. Inconsistent responses were identified by selecting questions which if answered consistently would have resulted in predictable answers from each item. For example, consistent respondents would have answered "never" when asked at what age they belonged to a gang and "no" in response to the item, "have you ever belonged to a gang?" On the *CYS*, 15 pairs of items compared the consistency of responses: high grades versus extremely high frequencies of absences, suspensions, and drug use (3 pairs); lifetime versus 30-day substance use (3 pairs); friends' behaviors and attitudes versus friends' drug use (2 pairs); gang membership (3 pairs); negative feelings about school versus looking forward to school (1 pair); grade level versus age (1 pair); and never used drugs versus reported drug use (2 pairs).

On the *SS/HS*, 17 similar pairs were used: greater frequency of risk behavior at school than lifetime frequency of that risk behavior (5 pairs); greater frequency of driving drunk than frequency of drinking alcohol (1 pair); reported behaviors, never in one question and always in another (4 pairs); greater frequency of carrying weapons at school than ever carried (4 pairs); actual grade versus reported grade (1 pair); and reported always feeling safe at school and reported not coming to school because they did NOT feel safe (2 pairs). On the *Perception Survey*, three pairs were used to compare use in the last year versus typical substance use for alcohol, marijuana, and tobacco.

Respondents that reported behaviors that were so extreme as to be logically implausible, if not impossible, were considered likely to be invalid. For example, students who reported that they had taken LSD 20 or more times in the last 30 days, or that they drank alcohol on school property more than 20 of the last 30 days were considered to be responding with implausibly extreme answers. On the *CYS*, three different types of measures were used to identify extreme responses: (1) used stimulants, LSD, cocaine, MDMA, or GHB 20+ times in 30 days (5 items); (2) reported high-risk behavior 40+ times in 30 days (8 items); and (3) positive behaviors were reported 40+ times in 30 days (2 items).

On the *SS/HS*, students who reported the highest possible frequency of a behavior were classified as extreme respondents: had 5 or more drinks in a row within a couple of hours (20+ times in last 30 days); in a physical fight on school property (12+ times in past 12 months); badly beaten up on school property, threatened with a gun on school property, injured with a gun on school property (very often[1] in past 12 months); seen other students badly beaten up on school property, threatened with a gun on school property, injured with a gun on school property (very often in last 12 months); running away from home (3+ times in past 12 months); been part of gang violence (3+ times in past 12 months); sold illegal drugs (3+ times in past 12 months). On the *Perception Survey*, three items regarding extreme levels of violence and substance were used.

A variable was created to count the number of inconsistent responses given by each student and another variable was created to count the number of times a student gave implausibly extreme answers (Table 1). These two counts were combined into a single measure[2] that counted the total number of extreme and inconsistent responses given by each student (Table 1). In order to demonstrate the effects of screening surveys for potentially invalid response patterns, we used the combined measure to classify surveys into three categories: not suspect, mildly

TABLE 1. Number of Responses Inconsistent, Extreme and Combined by Survey (*Safe Schools/Healthy Students* [*SS/HS*], *Colorado Youth Survey* [*CYS*], and *Perception*)

#	SS/HS Inconsistent n	SS/HS Extreme n	SS/HS Combined* n (%)	CYS Inconsistent n	CYS Extreme n	CYS Combined* n (%)	Perception Inconsistent n	Perception Extreme n	Perception Combined* n (%)
0	2334	2381	2127 (78.2)	2123	2099	1964 (84.4)	311	414	307 (58.9)
1	300	209	369 (13.6)	146	129	215 (10.7)	140	99	101 (19.4)
2	53	50	103 (3.8)	19	26	54 (2.6)	27	7	49 (9.4)
3	20	28	40 (1.5)	4	16	18 (0.9)	43	1	20 (3.8)
4	6	17	19 (0.7)	2	8	14 (0.4)	-	-	41 (7.9)
5	6	8	13 (0.5)	1	9	7 (0.3)	-	-	2 (0.4)
6	1	11	15 (0.6)	-	2	6 (0.1)	-	-	1 (0.2)
7	-	8	8 (0.3)	-	2	4 (0.2)	-	-	- -
8	-	8	14 (0.5)	-	1	3 (0.1)	-	-	- -
9	-	-	5 (0.2)	-	3	5 (0.1)	-	-	- -
10	-	-	5 (0.2)	-	-	2 (0.1)	-	-	- -
12	-	-	2 (0.1)	-	-	2 (0.1)	-	-	- -
16	-	-	- -	-	-	1 (0.0)	-	-	- -
TOTAL	2720	2720	2720 (100)	2295	2295	2295 (100)	521	521	521 (100)

* Counting the total number of extreme or inconsistent responses on each survey created the combined figures.

suspect, and highly suspect. Those students who gave no inconsistent or extreme answers were coded as "not suspect"; those students who gave 1 or 2 inconsistent or extreme answers were coded as "mildly suspect"; and those students who gave 3 or more inconsistent or extreme answers were coded as "highly suspect" (see Table 2).

Outcome Variables

We chose six outcome items for analysis. We selected commonly reported items that were worded similarly[3] on at least two of the three surveys. The six items reported include two risk behaviors: (1) ever "skipped" or "cut" a whole day of school in the last 30 days, and (2) ever consumed five or more drinks in a couple of hours during the last two (*SS/HS*) or four (*CYS*) weeks; two antisocial behaviors: (1) ever physically attacked someone in the past 30 days, and (2) ever taken a handgun to school in the past 30 days (*SS/HS*) or 12 months (*CYS*); one victimization item: ever been bullied or threatened physically attacked by another student on school property during the past 30 days; and one school climate measure: ever felt unsafe at school.

RESULTS

In this section, we first summarize the results of our checks for data quality and examine the influence of suspect responses on outcome variables. We then report the relationship found between training of administrators and data quality.

Suspect Responses

The combined proportions of inconsistent and illogically extreme responses can be found in Table 1. Of the three surveys examined, the

TABLE 2. Suspect Responses by Survey (*Safe Schools/Healthy Students* [*SS/HS*], *Colorado Youth Survey* [*CYS*], and *Perception*)

	SS/HS n (%)	CYS n (%)	Perception n (%)
Not Suspect	2127 (78.20)	1964 (85.58)	307 (58.9)
Mildly Suspect	472 (17.35)	269 (11.72)	150 (28.8)
Highly Suspect	121 (4.45)	62 (2.7)	64 (12.3)

Perception Survey had the highest overall rate of inconsistent and extreme responses. The percent of students giving any extreme or inconsistent responses was 41.1% on the *Perception Survey*, 21.8% on the *SS/HS*, and 15.6% on the *CYS* (Table 1). Once the surveys were categorized into three categories of suspect responses the pattern of inconsistency remained the same for the three surveys (Table 2). The proportion of highly suspect responses was greatest on the *Perception Survey* (12.3%), followed by the *SS/HS* (4.5%), and then *CYS* (2.7%).

Outcome Measures and Data Quality

How does the inclusion of suspect responses influence the interpretation of outcome measures? The overall proportion of suspect responses, 2.7% in the *CYS* and 4.4% in the *SS/HS*, might tempt one to believe that such small percentages of suspect answers would have a trivial influence on the interpretation of reported behaviors. Table 3 demonstrates

TABLE 3. Reported Risk Behaviors, Violence, and Victimization by Suspect Cases in *Colorado Youth Survey (CYS)*, *Safe Schools/Healthy Students (SS/HS)*, and *Perception Survey*

			Suspect Responses		
		TOTAL	Not Suspect	Mildly Suspect	Highly Suspect
		n (%)	n (%)	n (%)	n (%)
Skipped one or more days	CYS	432 (19.6)	294 (15.6)	98 (38.3)	40 (67.8)
of school in past 30 days*	SS/HS	589 (22.0)	362 (17.3)	151 (32.4)	76 (63.3)
	Perception	-	-	-	-
High-risk drinking (5+	CYS	593 (27.2)	413 (21.8)	129 (56.1)	51 (91.1)
drinks in a couple of hours)	SS/HS	650 (24.4)	409 (19.6)	157 (33.8)	84 (71.2)
in recent weeks*	Perception	-	-	-	-
Physically attacked or	CYS	242 (10.8)	133 (6.9)	65 (24.6)	44 (73.3)
harmed someone*	SS/HS	425 (15.8)	192 (9.9)	145 (31.2)	88 (74.6)
	Perception	65 (12.5)	35 (11.5)	22 (14.7)	8 (12.5)
Carried a handgun to	CYS	30 (1.3)	3 (0.2)	6 (2.3)	21 (34.4)
school*	SS/HS	86 (3.2)	3 (0.1)	23 (5.0)	60 (52.1)
	Perception	-	-	-	-
Physically attacked by	CYS	-	-	-	-
another student on school	SS/HS	862 (32.0)	600 (28.5)	188 (40.3)	74 (62.2)
property*	Perception	196 (37.8)	75 (24.5)	72 (48.3)	49 (76.6)
Feel unsafe at school*	CYS	379 (17.0)	270 (14.1)	74 (28.1)	35 (59.3)
	SS/HS	509 (18.9)	311 (14.7)	126 (27.0)	72 (60.0)
	Perception	43 (8.3)	23 (7.5)	11 (7.4)	9 (14.1)

* See Appendix for the exact wording of items.

that even the smallest percentage of suspect responses (2.7% on the *CYS*) overall can result in apparently inflated estimates of violence, risk behaviors, victimization, and poor school climate.

The results of screening out suspect responses are highly consistent. On all three surveys and on all items, inclusion of the students who gave highly inconsistent or extreme responses increased the estimates of risk behaviors, violent acts, antisocial behavior, and victimization (Table 3). Inclusion of suspect responses increased estimates of skipping school and high-risk drinking about 25%, and estimates of physical harm and bullying about 50%.

Screening for data quality had the most dramatic effect on estimates of gun carrying. The inclusion of suspect responses increased reports of carrying a gun from .2% to 1.3% on the *CYS* and from .1% to 3.2% on the *SS/HS* (Table 3). Logically, estimates of behaviors with very low incidence, say under 5%, will necessarily be more heavily influenced by the inclusion of suspect responses than behaviors with higher overall incidence, even when the overall percentage of potentially invalid surveys is only two or three percent of the entire sample.

On the *Perception Survey*, the conflation of the independent variable "school" with the dependent variable "suspect responses" heightened our conviction that researchers should screen for suspect responses before reporting results. If the proportion of students who reported having been bullied was reported without examining data quality, we would have claimed that bullying was reported by a greater proportion of students at City High School (45.7%) than at Valley High School (28.6%). However, when looking at only non-suspect responses, it appears that the more likely estimate of bullying at City High is about 25%, roughly equal to the percentage (26.3) at Valley High School.

Training of Survey Administrators and Suspect Responses

The analysis of individual items on both the *Perception Survey* and the *SS/HS* revealed surprisingly high proportions of extreme and inconsistent responses. These findings prompted an examination of factors that might explain those results. To examine the possibility of administrator effects, we made two comparisons. We first compared subsamples of the *Perception Survey* administered at two high schools with demographically similar populations, where the only difference was the training of the administrators. We also compared two similar risk behavior surveys, the *SS/HS* and the *CYS*, of similar length and content administered to comparable samples of students, but with different procedures of administration.

Perception Survey. After observing that over 50% of students at City High were inconsistent in their responses to two items regarding alcohol use, we investigated the distribution of suspect responses on the *Perception Survey.* Because this survey had been designed to guide prevention efforts at two different high schools, all analyses were run by the school, and, at first, it appeared that students at City High School (48.2% not suspect) were not responding as consistently as those at Valley High School (71.2% not suspect). However, once we reexamined the data after coding for administrator training, the percent of potentially invalid surveys was significantly lower (28%) among those surveys given by trained administrators at City High (Table 4).

Although we did not conduct a controlled experiment, we had three administrations of the survey to compare. When looking only at the surveys administered by the trained prevention specialists, the proportion of suspect responses from City High School was 26.8%, which was not significantly different from the proportion of suspect responses, 28.8%, from Valley High School, Somer's d, $p = .63$ (Table 4). Because the proportion of suspect responses at the two high schools where the survey was given by trained administrators was equivalent, we combined their responses and then compared their combined percentages of not suspect, mildly suspect, and highly suspect responses with the survey administered by untrained teachers at City High School, Pearson Chi-Square, $p < .001$. The percentage of mildly suspect responses was greater (35% versus 25%) and the per-

TABLE 4. *Perception Survey:* Suspect Responses by Training of Survey Administrators

	Untrained Administrators	Trained Administrators	
	City High School (spring 2002) *n* (%)	City High School (fall 2002) *n* (%)	Valley High School (spring 2002) *n* (%)
Not Suspect	71 (37.0)	63 (73.3)	173 (71.2)
Mildly Suspect	67 (34.9)[b]	22 (25.6)[a]	61 (25.1)
Highly Suspect	54 (28.1)	1 (1.2)	9 (3.7)

[a] Somer's *d*, $p = .624$, the percentages of not suspect, mildly suspect, and highly suspect responses at City High School in fall 2002 compared to the percentages of not suspect, mildly suspect, and highly suspect responses at Valley High School in spring 2002.

[b] Pearson Chi-Square, $p < .001$, the percentages of not suspect, mildly suspect, and highly suspect responses from the untrained administration (CHS spring 2002) compared to the trained administrations (CHS fall 2002 and VHS spring 2002).

centage of highly suspect responses was several times greater (28% versus 3%) in the sample given by untrained administrators (Table 4).

CYS and *SS/HS*. We observed that the proportion of suspect responses on the *CYS* was 12.4% in 1999, 11.8% in 2000, and 14.4% in 2001 (Table 5). Next, we compared the proportion of suspect responses between trained (*CYS*) and untrained (*SS/HS*) administrators. The survey given by untrained administrators had a higher proportion of suspect responses (21.8%) than the comparable survey administered by trained teachers, 14.4%, Pearson Chi-Square, $p < .001$ (Table 2).

DISCUSSION

This study supports the importance of performing checks for data quality of responses to student self-report surveys. We found proportions of inconsistent and illogically extreme responses ranging from 15% to 63% in some subsamples. The proportion of inconsistent and extreme responses was noteworthy because excluding those students who gave several inconsistent and/or extreme responses reduced the estimates of risk behaviors, antisocial behaviors, and victimization. Most importantly, the results demonstrated that even small percentages of suspect responses can dramatically alter the estimate of reported risk behaviors. On the *CYS*, which had the lowest percentage of highly suspect responses (2.7%), excluding only the highly suspect cases resulted in eliminating 70% of the total reports of carrying a gun to school. Our findings were consistent with the few other articles that have demonstrated that excluding cases that fail reliability or validity checks results in the reduction of reported violence and risk behaviors (Cornell & Loper, 1998; Rosenblatt & Furlong, 1997).

The methods we used for identifying inconsistent and extreme responses can be easily replicated with many other surveys, as most of the

TABLE 5. *Colorado Youth Survey* (*CYS*): Suspect Responses by Year

	1999 n (%)	2000 n (%)	2001 n (%)
Not Suspect	1744 (87.6)	2198 (88.2)	1964 (85.6)
Mildly Suspect	214 (10.8)	258 (10.4)	269 (11.7)
Highly Suspect	32 (1.6)	36 (1.4)	62 (2.7)

Note. No significant differences were found in this table, X^2 (2) = 7.95, p = .02; proportions of suspect responses compared across 1999, 2000, and 2001.

commonly used school climate and risk behavior surveys ask a number of questions that can be cross-referenced with each other to detect inconsistency. Surveys that include extraordinarily high frequency ranges for behavioral questions can be especially useful in detecting implausible and impossible reports. Running both of these checks picks up students who tend to give only extreme responses as well as students who answer inconsistently. Using these two checks in combination allows researchers to identify students who gave multiple responses that suggest their responses may be invalid, rather than relying on only one or two questions as validity checks.

Data quality can be affected by a variety of factors including administration procedures. Our results suggested that administration procedures may have increased the proportion of suspect responses. Evidence for this was strongest on the *Perception Survey* where the survey was administered at the same high school by both trained and untrained administrators. It is possible that something other than administrator training might better explain the high proportions of suspect responses in the first sample from City High School; however, the similarity in proportion of suspect responses in the second sample from City High School and the sample from Valley High School suggests that difference in suspect responses at the two high schools is not likely the result of any demographic differences between the two schools. Comments from students, teachers, and school administrators following the survey administrations lent additional support for the argument that the administrator can influence students' motivations to answer truthfully and consistently. One of the teachers who administered the *Perception Survey* with the highest proportion of inconsistent and extreme responses was known to have poor rapport with students and consistent difficulties maintaining authority in the classroom.

Comparisons made between the *CYS* and *SS/HS* raised our concern that training of administrators may have contributed to the higher proportion of suspect responses to the *SS/HS*; however, this hypothesis could not be confirmed with available data. Other possible explanations include differences in the surveys themselves, the items used to detect inconsistent and extreme responses, and differences in staff and student cultures at the various schools. Suspicion that training of administrators may have influenced the proportion of suspect responses was heightened by comments from students, teachers, and school principals. The researchers received no negative comments regarding the four administrations of the *CYS*. Despite the similarity of the *SS/HS* to the *CYS*, the researchers received numerous negative comments from students, teachers, principals, and even parents regarding the *SS/HS*. Students reported that they perceived the survey to be insulting, junior high school teachers reported that the questions were inappropriate for their students, one principal indicated that he did not direct his students to answer sincerely, and parents complained that their students were required to take surveys with that content in the schools. Although these comments cannot confirm our hypothesis regarding the training of administrators, they suggest the need for research on the effect of survey format and training of administrators on respondent motivation and survey results.

Another pertinent issue to consider is the potential of suspect responses to be a confounding variable, thus influencing the analysis of risk factors. Our findings suggested that when any independent variable (gender, age, grade, race, school, or district) is correlated with suspect responses, potentially invalid response patterns could confound efforts to compare groups of students by age, classroom, gender, or school. Before screening for suspect responses, it appeared that students at one high school were 60% more likely to be bullied than students at the comparison school. Once we controlled for suspect responses, equal proportions of students reported having been bullied and the relationship between school and bullying disappeared. This finding reinforced the importance of running reliability and validity checks before conducting any other analysis of self-report data.

The study of school climate and youth violence could benefit from the development of standards for survey administration like those that have been adopted in public opinion polling. We recommend that survey researchers include the results of checks for inconsistent and extreme responses in their findings and that journal editors request this information be included in all submitted articles. Future research should examine the effect of administrator training and classroom rapport on survey results. Results of such research could be used for the development of survey administration standards and would likely improve the quality of data available to local and national policy makers.

Researchers should be cautious about removing those cases that fail standard reliability and validity checks. While it is possible to identify those students who gave inconsistent or implausibly extreme answers, it is not possible to know which of those responses are true responses, which may be exaggerations, or which may be understatements. The removal of inconsistent and extreme cases may increase the researcher's confidence that reported behaviors are true behaviors, but it may also inadvertently bias the data toward more normative behavior. If there is a true correlation between the tendency to answer inconsistently or extremely and to engage in risk behaviors, removing those students who fail reliability and validity checks may also remove many of the true incidences of risk behavior. This dilemma highlights one of the limitations of survey data for understanding rare events. Many school climate and violence prevention surveys include questions about rare events that would likely be better studied through other methods or mixed method design.

Perhaps the most important reason to check and report reliability and validity for self-report surveys is the propensity of false information to create exaggerated public concern for extremely rare events. Sociologists have documented a variety of cases where public fear is greatly disproportional to actual risk (Best & Horiuchi, 1985). Especially in regards to school violence, the media has contributed to exaggerated public fear for the safety of students in schools (Glassner, 1999; Mulvey & Cauffman, 2001). Given the nature of the data reported in school climate and risk behavior surveys, researchers have an ethical responsibility to be sure that the data are as trustworthy as possible before reporting them. While self-report surveys will likely continue to be an economical method for gathering violence and risk behavior data from students, their value is fragile unless data quality issues are systematically addressed in administration, interpretation, reporting, and publishing of results.

NOTES

1. This survey included 15 items about crime and violence experienced during the past 12 months; the responses categories were "never," "once," "several times," and "very often."

2. The combined measure was created to simplify analysis for the purposes of this article, the differences in these two types of checks would be an interesting topic for further investigation. Potentially invalid responses may be caught by either the extreme responses checks or the inconsistent checks. Combining the counts of extreme and inconsistent responses allowed us to identify students who gave multiple responses that are potentially invalid, but who may have not been identified as giving multiple inconsistent responses or multiple extreme responses.

3. See Appendix for the exact wording of items and responses included in analysis. The intention of including similar items from different surveys was to take advantage of available data to demonstrate the influence of suspect responses on the estimates of commonly reported behaviors. No inferences are made about the comparability of the different measures between surveys.

REFERENCES

Best, J., & Horiuchi, G. T. (1985). The razor blade in the apple: The social construction of urban legends. *Social Problems, 32,* 488-499.

Brener, N. D., Kann, L., McManus, T., Kinchen, S. A., Sundberg, E. C., & Ross, J. G. (2002). Reliability of the 1999 youth risk behavior survey questionnaire. *Journal of Adolescent Health, 31,* 336-342.

Cornell, D. G., & Loper, A. B. (1998). Assessment of violence and other high-risk behaviors with a school survey. *School Psychology Review, 27*(2), 317-330.

Curry, G. D. (2000). Self-reported gang involvement and officially recorded delinquency. *Criminology, 38*(4), 1253-1274.

Deming, W. E. (1970). On errors in surveys. In N. K. Denzin, *Sociological methods* (pp. 320-337). Chicago: Aldine Publishing.

Elliot, D. S., Huizinga, D., & Menard, S. (1989). *Multiple problem youth: Delinquency, substance use, and mental health problems.* New York: Springer-Verlag.

Fetters, W. B., Stowe, P. S., & Owings, J. A. (1984). *High school and beyond: A national longitudinal study for the 1980's. Quality of responses of high school students to questionnaire items* (NCES Report 84-216). Washington, DC: National Center for Education Statistics.

Finkelhor, D. (1998). A comparison of the responses of preadolescents and adolescents in a national victimization survey. *Journal of Interpersonal Violence, 13*(3), 362-382.

Glassner, B. (1999). *The culture of fear: Why Americans are afraid of the wrong things.* New York: Basic Books.

Graham, J. W., Roberts, M. M., Tatterson, J. W., & Johnston, S. E. (2002). Data quality of an alcohol-related harm prevention program. *Evaluation Review, 26*(2), 147-189.

Groves, R. M. (1987). Research on survey data quality. *Public Opinion Quarterly, 51*, S156-S172.

Huizinga, D., & Elliott, D. S. (1986). Reassessing the reliability and validity of self-report delinquency measures. *Journal of Quantitative Criminology, 2*(4), 293-327.

Li, T., Trivedi, P. K., & Guo, J. (2003). Modeling response bias in count: A structural approach with an application to the National Crime Victimization Survey data. *Sociological Methods & Research, 31*(4), 514-544.

Mulvey, E. P., & Cauffman, E. (2001). The inherent limits of predicting school violence. *American Psychologist, 56*, 797-802.

Orne, M. T. (1970). On the social psychology of the psychological experiment: With particular reference to demand characteristics and their implications. In N. K. Denzin, *Sociological methods* (pp. 320-337). Chicago: Aldine.

Rosenblatt, J. A., & Furlong, M. J. (1997). Assessing the reliability and validity of student self-reports of campus violence. *Journal of Youth and Adolescence, 26*(2), 187-202.

Schiltz, M. E. (1988). Professional standards for survey research. *Research in Higher Education, 28*(1), 67-75.

Schumacher, S., & McMillan, J. H. (1993). *Research in education: A conceptual introduction.* New York: Harper Collins College Publishers.

Tanur, J. M. (1994, May 25). The trustworthiness of survey research. *The Chronicle of Higher Education, 38*, B1-B3.

Weisberg, H. F., Krosnick, J. A., & Bowen, B. D. (1996). *An introduction to survey research, polling, and data analysis.* Thousand Oaks: Sage Publications.

APPENDIX

Question Wording and Responses Included in Table 3

Survey	Question	Responses Reported in Table 3
Skipped one or more days of school in past 30 days.		
CYS	In the last 4 weeks, how many whole days of school have you missed because you because you skipped or "cut"?	1, 2, 3, 4-5, 6-10, 11+
SS/HS	During the last 30 days, how many whole days of school have you missed because you skipped or "cut"?	1, 2, 3, 4-5, 6-10, 11+
Perception	----	
High-risk drinking (5+ drinks in a couple of hours) in recent weeks.		
CYS	Think back over the last 2 weeks. How many times have you had 5 or more alcoholic drinks in a row?	1, 2, 3-5, 6-9, 10+
SS/HS	During the last 30 days, on how many days did you have 5 or more drinks of alcohol in a row—that is, within a couple of hours?	1, 2, 3-4, 6-9, 10-19, 20+
Perception	-----	
Physically attacked or harmed someone.		
CYS	How many times in the past year (the last 12 months) have you attacked someone with the idea of seriously hurting them?	1-2, 3-5, 6-9, 10-19, 20-29, 30-39, 40+
SS/HS	During the past 12 months, how often have you hurt someone enough to need bandages or a doctor?	once, twice, 3 or 4, 5 or more
Perception	How often in the past 30 days have you attacked someone physically?	1-2, 3-5, 6+
Carried a handgun to school.		
CYS	How many times in the past year (the last 12 months) have you taken a handgun to school?	1-2, 3-5, 6-9, 10-19, 20-29, 30-39, 40+
SS/HS	During the past 30 days, on how many days did you carry a gun on school property?	1, 2 or 3, 4 or 5, 6 or more
Perception	-----	
Physically attacked by another student on school property.		
CYS	-----	
SS/HS	During the past 12 months, how often have you been hit, kicked, or pushed by a student on school property?	once, several times, very often
Perception	How often in the past 30 days have you been attacked physically by another student?	1-2 times, 3-5 times, 6+ times
Feel unsafe at school.		
CYS	How safe do you feel at school?	very safe, somewhat safe
SS/HS	How often do you feel unsafe when you are at school?	some days, most days, everyday
Perception	Which statement best describes your feelings of safety at school?	"I feel somewhat unsafe," "I feel very unsafe"

An Examination of the Reliability, Data Screening Procedures, and Extreme Response Patterns for the Youth Risk Behavior Surveillance Survey

Michael J. Furlong
Jill D. Sharkey
Michael P. Bates
Douglas C. Smith

SUMMARY. This article explores psychometric characteristics of the Youth Risk Behavior Surveillance Survey (YRBS), one of the most widely used instruments to assess the prevalence of violent and other high-risk behaviors in secondary school settings. Response patterns

Michael J. Furlong is Professor in the Counseling/Clinical/School Psychology Program, University of California, Santa Barbara.

Jill D. Sharkey and Michael P. Bates are doctoral researchers, University of California, Santa Barbara.

Douglas C. Smith is Associate Professor in the Counselor Education Program, University of Hawaii, Manoa.

Address correspondence to: Michael Furlong, UCSB, GGSE, Center for School-Based Youth Development, Santa Barbara, CA 93106-9490 (E-mail: mfurlong@education.ucsb.edu).

This article was supported in part by a grant from the Don and Marilyn Gevirtz Funds for Excellence Initiative.

[Haworth co-indexing entry note]: "An Examination of the Reliability, Data Screening Procedures, and Extreme Response Patterns for the Youth Risk Behavior Surveillance Survey." Furlong, Michael J. et al. Co-published simultaneously in *Journal of School Violence* (The Haworth Press, Inc.) Vol. 3, No. 2/3, 2004, pp. 109-130; and: *Issues in School Violence Research* (ed: Michael J. Furlong et al.) The Haworth Press, Inc., 2004, pp. 109-130. Single or multiple copies of this article are available for a fee from The Haworth Document Delivery Service [1-800-HAWORTH, 9:00 a.m. - 5:00 p.m. (EST). E-mail address: docdelivery@haworthpress.com].

http://www.haworthpress.com/web/JSV
© 2004 by The Haworth Press, Inc. All rights reserved.
Digital Object Identifier: 10.1300/J202v03n02_07

were analyzed for a subset of 414 youths who indicated that they had carried a weapon to school six or more times during the preceding 30 days, and were compared to a matched sample of youths randomly selected from the 13,610 participants in the 2001 national administration of the YRBS. Results indicated that extreme responders to the weapon-carrying item were considerably more likely than their counterparts to respond in an extreme fashion to *all* YRBS items, including risk items pertaining to school (e.g., physical fights on school property) and outside school (e.g., alcohol consumption) factors, as well as positive health behaviors (e.g., healthy eating habits). Overall, the results suggest an extreme response bias among some participants that may impact the validity of the YRBS instrument. More specifically, presence of this response bias may inflate estimates of the prevalence of school violence and related concerns. These findings are discussed in light of the need to carefully examine individual response patterns on future administrations of the YRBS in an effort to ensure maximum instrument utility. *[Article copies available for a fee from The Haworth Document Delivery Service: 1-800-HAWORTH. E-mail address: <docdelivery@haworthpress.com> Website: <http://www.HaworthPress.com> © 2004 by The Haworth Press, Inc. All rights reserved.]*

KEYWORDS. Psychometric, school violence, weapons, school safety, Youth Risk Behavior Surveillance Survey

The Youth Risk Behavior Surveillance Survey (YRBS) was developed in the late 1980s by the Center for Disease Control and Prevention (CDC) to conduct epidemiological studies of the prevalence of risk behaviors that contributed to injury (Kolbe, Kann, & Collins, 1993). Of particular concern at that time was a rapid increase in substance use and homicides among adolescents. The YRBS was first administered in 1990 using a multilevel sampling procedure involving schools, classrooms, and specific students within classrooms (Brener, Collins, Kann, Warren, & Williams, 1995). Over the years, the YRBS has been modified to expand its item content in response to rising social concerns. Among these concerns was the growing visibility of violence on America's school campuses. Beginning in 1993, and biennially thereafter, items pertaining to violence-related behaviors at school were added. Despite widespread use of the YRBS in school violence research (e.g., Coggeshall & Kingery, 2001; Furlong, Bates, & Smith, 2001), there has been limited discussion of its characteristics as a school violence and safety research instrument.

The YRBS is and will continue to be a meaningful contributor to school violence research; however, only one study has examined the reliability of the YRBS school violence items, and it found only marginal support for their reliability. Related research has shown that data screening is important and should be conducted on large-scale surveys, especially if it addresses inconsistent *and* implausible responding. The YRBS has established procedures (not typically mentioned in published studies involving the YRBS) for data cleansing aimed at inconsistent and invalid responses, but does not check for implausible response patterns. First, this article provides an overview of psychometric information published regarding the YRBS, focusing specifically on those items that query school-related behaviors. Understanding the psychometric properties of the YRBS is crucial because it is a prominent source of data on the prevalence of school violence and, specifically, the incidence of school weapon possession (Furlong, Bates, Smith, & Sharkey, 2004; Furlong et al., 2001). Second, we examine one form of implausible responding–extreme responding. We explore whether or not extreme responses to individual items can be explained, at least in part, by a tendency to select the most extreme response options (*extreme response bias*). To do this, we conduct an exploratory analysis of the 2001 YRBS database examining the response profiles of those students who indicated they had possession of a weapon at school six or more times in the preceding 30 days, the most extreme response option. This analysis provides an opportunity to examine the response patterns of those students who presumably pose a great risk of harm to students and others on school campuses and to assess the veracity of these self-reports.

USES AND PROMINENCE OF THE YRBS

The Youth Risk Behavior Surveillance Survey is arguably the single most widely used source of information about the incidence of high-risk behaviors among adolescents. It has provided information for numerous studies of adolescent *steroid use* (DuRant et al., 1993; Miller, Barnes, Sabo, Melnick, & Farrell, 2002); *same-sex behavior* (Faulkner & Cranston, 1998); *sexual risk behavior* (Hennessy, 1999; Hou & Basen-Engquist, 1997); *pregnancy* (Pierre, Shrier, Emans, & DuRant, 1998); *suicidal behavior* (Cleary, 2000); *diet, exercise, and weight control* (Becher et al., 1999; Felts, Parrillo, Chenier, & Dunn, 1996; Garry,

Morrissey, & Whetstone, 2003; Pesa & Turner, 2001); *tobacco use* (Everett, Giovino, Warren, Crossett, & Kann, 1998; Melnick, Miller, Sabo, Farrell, & Barnes, 2001; Merrill, Kleber, Shwartz, Liu, & Lewis, 1999); and *substance use* (Shrier, Emans, Woods, & DuRant, 1997). A measure of the YRBS's status is also its prevalence in youth surveillance studies in other countries (Gwede et al., 2001; Page, & Zarco, 2001) and its use to inform regional and national policy in the U.S. (DeVoe et al., 2002; Luke, Stamatakis, & Brownson, 2000; U.S. Departments of Education and Justice, 2000). As the YRBS has reached this level of prominence in the assessment of youth risk behaviors, its use has expanded beyond its original national epidemiological purpose to assess special populations such as *alternative high school students* (Grunbaum, Lowry, & Kann, 2001), *Asian and Pacific Islanders* (Grunbaum, Lowry, Kann, & Pateman, 2000), *youths with depression symptoms* (Light, 2000), *American Indians* (Nelson, Moon, Holtzman, Smith, & Siegel, 1997); and *youths with serious emotional disturbance* (Valois, Bryant, Rivard, & Hinkle, 1997).

School Violence Research Using the YRBS

Among the YRBS youth risk domains that have drawn intense scrutiny from researchers, the public, and policy makers are the incidences and patterns of youth aggression and violence-risk behaviors. Most of these studies have focused on the correlates of fighting and weapon carrying that could have occurred on or off the school campus (e.g., Hill, 1998; Lowry, Powell, Kann, Collins, & Kolbe, 1998; Orpinas, Basen-Engquist, Grunbaum, & Parcel, 1995). However, with the public availability of the biennial YRBS databases, it has also been used to examine the incidence of aggression and violence as it specifically pertains to school campuses (Coggeshall & Kingery, 2001; Furlong et al., 2001, 2004). In some instances, YRBS items have been combined to form school violence subscales or indices and used in secondary analyses (e.g., Furlong et al., 2001). As the YRBS database is used increasingly in ways for which it was not designed or originally intended, it is imperative that efforts continue to explore its psychometric characteristics.

Psychometric Characteristics of the YRBS

Given the prominence of the YRBS in school violence research and its influence on safe schools public policy, it might be assumed that it has undergone careful psychometric analysis. This, however, is not the case. Brener et al. (1995) first examined the stability of YRBS responses by using the March 1992 version to a nonrandom sample of youth. This version did not contain items related to risk, safety, or violence behaviors that occurred on a school campus. Klein, Graff, Santelli, Allan, and Elster (2001) also examined the measurement characteristics of the YRBS, but did not evaluate any of the school items. Brener et al. (2002) completed the only study to date that has examined the reliability of the YRBS items that inquire about school-associated behaviors. This study examined the responses of 4,619 of 6,802 eligible students who completed the YRBS twice over a two-week time period. Responses to all items were converted into binary format in order to compute a kappa statistic, a measure of response consistency that is corrected for chance agreement. Table 1 shows the kappa statistics and the time 1 and time 2 incidences for each school-associated YRBS item as presented by Brener et al. (2002). The four YRBS items that directly assess school violence content had kappas ranging from .406 to .678, and the incidence of one (students indicating they had been "Injured in a physical fight 1 time in the past 12 months") was significantly higher at time 2 compared to time 1.

Though Brener et al. (2002) concluded that the YRBS was a reliable instrument, there were several methodological questions with the study, including (a) interpretation of kappas from items with different reference time frames (e.g., past 30 days and past 12 months), (b) using a 14-day (average) retest period for items with 30-day or 12-month reference time frames, (c) appropriateness of the kappa statistic, (d) exclusion of inconsistent responses prior to analysis, and (e) conversion of responses to binary format. As a result, this analysis likely generated the most favorable possible results for test-retest reliability, and yet the kappa values for the school items were still marginal at best.

Data Preparation and Editing

Although not reported in any YRBS published study, the raw data obtained from the national survey process, as would be true of any large school-based survey, are subject to a variety of data check and editing procedures. The 2003 YRBS undergoes multiple consistency checks (J. Grunbaum, May 16, 2003, personal communication). For example, youths are asked to indicate if they have carried any weapon (anywhere) in the past 30 days and if they had carried a gun (anywhere) in the past 30 days. Clearly, a gun is a subclass of all weapon possession; therefore, it would be an inconsistent response if youths indicate that they carried a

TABLE 1. Test-Retest Item Kappa Statistics for 1999 YRBS School-Associated Items and Available Nonschool Parallel Worded Items and Time 1 and Time 2 Prevalence Estimates

1999 YRBS Item	Item Kappa		Prevalence (%) [a]	
	Parallel [b]	School	Time 1	Time 2 [c]
School Safety Items				
Carried weapon on school property ≥ 1 day during the past 30 days	**65.7**	57.7	5.1	5.7
Felt too unsafe to go to school ≥ 1 day during the past 30 days	-	42.0	5.5	5.0
Threatened or injured with weapon on school property ≥ 1 time in the past 12 months	-	40.6	7.3	5.9
In a physical fight on school property ≥ 1 time in past 12 months	**67.8**	64.4	13.1	12.4
School Risk Behaviors				
Smoked cigarettes ≥ 1 day on school property during the past 30 days	**81.9**	71.4	9.7	9.1
Used smokeless tobacco on school property ≥ 1 day during the past 30 days	**71.4**	60.4	3.9	3.9
Drank alcohol on school property ≥ 1 day during the past 30 days	**70.9**	49.4	3.9	4.1
Used marijuana on school property during the past 30 days	**76.0**	59.1	5.5	5.3
Offered, sold, or given illegal drugs on school property during the past 12 months	-	52.2	23.0	21.9
School Health Behaviors				
Attend physical education class ≥ 1 day a week	-	84.8	62.4	56.8
Exercise ≥ 20 minutes during physical education class	-	41.1	72.3	69.0
Played on ≥ 1 sports team during the past 12 months	-	56.2	54.6	53.3
Ever been taught about AIDS or HIV in school	-	23.6	85.0	86.2

[a] Prevalence is the weighted percentage of youth who engaged in the behavior regardless of frequency.
[b] Parallel YRBS items asked the same question but did not specify the school context. These questions presumably ask about illicit responses about risk behaviors in both nonschool and school settings.
[c] Average time from time 1 to time 2 was 14 days.
Source: Brener et al. (2002).

gun more often than a weapon during the past month. In fact, the CDC checks these two items, and the responses of youths who indicate that they carried a gun more often than a weapon are assigned a missing value for both items. Altogether 225 such response consistency checks are made with the 2003 High School YRBS, and similar procedures have been used with previous YRBS administrations (J. Grunbaum, June 24, 2003, personal communication). When inconsistent responses are obtained, the values of both items are recoded as missing. There is no limit to the number of values that can be recoded as missing, and there is no way to know from the YRBS public access data file if a missing value was due to a nonresponse or response inconsistency (J. Grunbaum, June 25, 2003, personal communication).

In addition, youths are dropped from the sample (case-wise deletion) if they (a) do not respond to 20 items when 55 or more items are used, (b) do not respond to 15 or more items when 54 or fewer items are used, (c) give the same numbered response option 15 or more times in a row with 55 or more items, or (d) give the same numbered response option 12 or more times in a row when 54 or fewer items are used. These case-wise deletions are an historical procedure used to screen for obvious response sets and multiple omissions (J. Grunbaum, June 24, 2003, personal communication). Of note, however, is that the number of response options for each item influences this editing procedure. Students' response patterns can change merely because the number of available options changes. Thus, a student who simply selects the highest response option for each item would not be eliminated because there is no sequence of YRBS items for which the maximum response option is the same for 12 or 15 items in a row. Consequently, this case-elimination rule can only exclude cases in which the student is repeatedly selecting responses reflecting a lower frequency of behavior (i.e., a, b, or c).

Finally, although many response consistency checks are made, many important checks are not included. For example, the frequency of gun possession (anywhere) is checked against the school weapon possession items, but no check is made to assess if responses to the school weapon-carrying item is consistent with the weapon-carrying item that does not specify location and would therefore include weapon-carrying anywhere, both school and nonschool locations. Hence, if perfectly consistent, no youth should indicate that he or she carried a weapon in school more often during the past 30 days than in the nonspecific weapon-carrying item.

Veracity of Student Self-Report School Violence Data

Efforts are made to examine the quality of the responses provided by youths to the YRBS. In assessing these procedures, it is instructive to consider what other research has found about the veracity of student self-reports of campus violence and safety matters. Several studies have examined the effects of inconsistent and unreliable data on estimates of school violence prevalence.

In one study, Rosenblatt and Furlong (1997) examined response consistency of self-reported school violence victimization. They made a comparison between two items that asked about feelings of personal safety at school: "I feel perfectly safe at this school" and "I do not feel safe at this school" (from the *National Educational Longitudinal Study* questionnaire, Green et al., 1995). If a student responded consistently, agreement on one item should correspond to disagreement on the other item, or the reverse. If responses to these two personal safety items were the same (either *agree* or *disagree* to both items), the student was assigned to the Rejected group. One validity check item representing an improbable situation ("I took ten field trips in the previous month") was randomly embedded among 21 other items pertaining to campus violence. Students who answered "yes" to this implausible item were considered to be answering questions haphazardly and were assigned to the Rejected group. Inconsistent responders were found to have higher scores on an index of school violence victimization and on perceived danger of the school environment. Only 2% of the inconsistent group reported that they had they no victimization compared to 15% of the consistent responders. In addition, about 30% failed to pass the three validity checks (i.e., more than 4 missing, obvious response sets, and out-of-range responses).

In another investigation, Cornell and Loeper (1998) suggested that the case-wise elimination in school safety surveys may be a concern and that few school-based surveys specifically explore for "exaggerated and careless reporting" (p. 319). Inherent in their analysis was the assumption that among the various sources of inaccuracies in school safety self-reports is that youth may respond carelessly (intentionally or not) and that their responses may be affected by exaggerated response tendencies (faking good or bad). They provided a detailed examination of the influences of these types of responses using a sample of more than 10,000 Virginia students in grades 7, 9, and 11. These students were asked to comment on their school safety experiences during the previous 30-day period. Responses were examined against 8 invalidity criteria under 3 categories: missing or inappropriate responses to key demographic items, responding "no" to one of two global validity check items ("I am reading this survey carefully" and "I am telling the truth on this survey"), and indicating that they had engaged in 6 high-risk behaviors in or out of school. Using these case-wise selection rules, 24.2% of the sample was placed into an invalid group and their responses compared with those students who passed all validity check responses. Strikingly, it was found that invalid responders were much more likely to report that they had engaged in various high-risk behaviors at school. For example, 9.9% of the valid responders reported carrying a weapon (not a gun) to school in the past 30 days compared to 53.4% of the invalid responders. In addition, the rate of weapon carrying was higher (35.8%) even for those youth who only answered "no" to one of the global validity check items.

Based on these results, Cornell and Loeper (1998) recommended ". . . careful screening of school surveys to eliminate forms which may have been completed in a careless or intentionally invalid a manner. Because high-risk behavior such as weapon carrying and fighting at school occurs in a relatively small proportion of students, the inclusion of carelessly completed forms will lead to inflated estimates of their prevalence. Moreover, some students will intentionally exaggerate their claims in involvement in high-risk behaviors" (p. 328).

These early investigations of school violence measurement issues provided evidence supporting the validity of using student self-reports of violence but also raised some methodological questions about possible sources of response invalidity that, if not attended to, may overstate the frequency of violence-associated behaviors on school campuses. These studies did not examine the YRBS per se; consequently, it is important to examine what is known about the reliability and validity of the YRBS.

METHOD

2001 YRBS Public Domain Database

In 2001, the YRBS national sampling process produced 16,398 cases of which 13,601 were usable. This means that the cases passed the liberal response pattern and minimum number of items completed casewise deletion criteria. These two criteria alone eliminated 17% of the cases. In addition, 1 out of 4 schools did not participate; thus, the reported response rate of 63% actually underestimates the proportion of students who were selected in the original sampling pool. Furthermore, the response inconsistency data editing procedures were then applied to these data. Responses could be coded as missing either because a youth did not complete the item or their response was invalidated by one of the data editing checks, in which both comparison items were coded as missing.[1] From the public access databases, there is no way to ascertain the source of missing data for any particular item (J. Grunbaum, June 25, 2003, personal communication). In addition, items for which consistency checks were made, as might be expected, had more missing values. Of interest is that the consistency checks were almost exclusively for nonschool items, with school items being coded missing if they were inconsistent with a related nonschool item.[2] For instance, in the 2001 YRBS the youths were questioned regarding the frequency of smoking within a 30-day period not only in general, but also specific to the school setting. Smoking in general should be equal to or greater than smoking at school. When this comparison is made, 641 of the general item responses and 221 of the school responses were recoded to missing due to inconsistent responses. There was only one consistency check for school-related behaviors. A question regarding the number of days a student participated in physical education (P.E.) classes in a week was compared with a question regarding the average amount of time spent in that same class. Some students indicated that they did not have P.E., but then indicated that they spent some time engaged in P.E. activities. Also, some youths indicated that they had P.E. classes, but did not spend any time in the class. These inconsistent responses were coded as missing, resulting in 1,398 and 1,582 recoded missing responses for the two school P.E. items, respectively.

YRBS 2001 Participants

The YRBS data files and corresponding codebooks were obtained via the Internet from the Centers for Disease Control and Prevention. Data from the 2001 national administration were used. The 2001 YRBS is made up of 13,601 students, of whom 51% were female and 49% were male. In terms of ethnicity, students were 2% American Indian, 3% Asian American, 20% African American, 22% Latino American, 1% Pacific Islander, 47% European American, and 5% multiethnic. These students were spread fairly evenly between grades 9 (25%), 10 (25%), 11 (26%) and 12 (24%). Of this total group, 426 (3%) responded that, during the past 30 days, they brought a weapon, such as a gun, knife, or club, on school property 6 or more times. In order to further examine the response style of this subsection of youths, this group was matched by gender and grade with a random sample of youths from the remainder of the YRBS sample.

Target Group. The target group consisted of those youths who responded to the most extreme response (6 or more days) on YRBS item 15, "During the past 30 days, on how many days did you carry a weapon such as a gun, knife, or club on school property?" Because the target sample was matched by gender and grade, youths with missing responses to these questions were dropped ($n = 12$), leaving a total sample of 414 youths. Of these, 23% were female, 77% male, 20% in grade 9,

22% in grade 10, 29% in grade 11, and 27% in grade 12. In addition, this sample consisted of 4% American Indians, 2% Asian Americans, 13% African Americans, 15% Latino Americans, 1% Pacific Islanders, 57% European Americans, and 8% multiethnic youths.

Matched Group. The matched group was randomly selected from the larger group of youths who did not give the most extreme response regarding weapon possession at school (but could have indicated some lower level of school weapon possession) and matched by gender and grade after deleting cases missing gender or grade ($n = 231$). Thus, this group had the same proportion of males to females and the same proportion within grade level. In terms of ethnicity, this group consisted of 2% American Indians, 3% Asian Americans, 18% African Americans, 20% Latino Americans, 1% Pacific Islanders, 48% European Americans, and 6% multiethnic youths.

RESULTS

Results of descriptive and multivariate statistics are illustrated in Table 2. Appendix A provides a list of items included in the analyses along with the most extreme response choice. As can be seen in Table 2, youths in the target group had significantly higher mean scores on almost all of the items, including two health items. Responses for youths in the target group were not statistically different from youths in comparison group with regards to eating, exercising, and participating on sports teams.

Items were grouped into three categories of interest: school, risk, and health. School items included all school risk factors on the YRBS. Risk items included a sampling of unhealthy behaviors (e.g., heroin use), and health items included a sampling of healthy behaviors (e.g., eating carrots). Multivariate analyses were conducted for each group of items in order to determine whether or not responding patterns differed significantly between youths who chose the most extreme weapon response and the randomly selected matched group. Youths who chose the most extreme weapon response had significantly higher levels of school risk behaviors, $F(7, 710) = 17.000$, $p = .001$, general risk behaviors, $F(5, 675) = 16.635$, $p = .001$, and health behaviors, $F(4, 764) = 3.172$, $p = .013$.

As another level of analysis, we tallied the number of students who responded with the most extreme response for each item. This proportion is reported in Table 2 as *Pext (%)*. A larger proportion of target youths than comparison group youths chose the extreme response for all items

TABLE 2. Weapons Responders versus Comparison Sample: Descriptive and Multivariate Statistics

		Target Sample				Comparison Sample					
Item	Range	N	M	SD	Pext (%)[1]	N	M	SD	Pext (%)[1]	F	p
Target Item											
15 (weapon)	1-5	414	5.0	0	100.0	414	1.08	.40	0.0	-	-
School Items											
16 (unsafe)	1-5	414	1.52	1.28	10.6	413	1.11	.51	1.0	29.356	.000
17 (threat)	1-8	413	2.34	2.43	12.6	414	1.14	.65	0.2	75.966	.000
20 (fight)	1-8	404	2.28	2.23	9.7	408	1.23	.73	0.0	61.750	.000
34 (smoke)	1-7	394	2.42	2.31	15.5	408	1.30	1.06	2.0	63.303	.000
38 (chew)	1-7	390	2.01	2.04	11.5	385	1.21	.87	0.8	46.884	.000
44 (drink)	1-7	389	1.78	1.66	6.2	408	1.07	.36	0.0	61.125	.000
48 (pot)	1-6	401	1.97	1.70	10.8	408	1.17	.67	0.7	55.467	.000
Risk Items											
26 (suicide)	1-5	378	1.62	1.30	10.8	343	1.09	.47	0.9	48.140	.000
43 (drink)	1-7	392	2.86	2.09	9.7	408	1.89	1.45	1.2	60.408	.000
52 (glue)	1-6	400	1.56	1.41	7.0	404	1.09	.49	0.5	34.266	.000
53 (heroin)	1-6	407	1.57	1.45	8.1	411	1.08	.51	0.7	31.720	.000
55 (steroid)	1-6	406	1.66	1.51	7.9	410	1.12	.57	0.5	36.518	.000
Health Items											
77 (carrots)	1-7	399	1.96	1.46	3.8	387	1.70	1.12	1.3	8.789	.003
79 (milk)	1-7	411	3.80	2.08	17.0	406	3.46	1.89	9.9	4.614	.032
80 (exercise)	1-8	396	4.92	2.74	32.8	388	4.74	2.55	23.2	.772	.380
86 (teams)	1-4	406	2.03	1.13	16.5	399	2.06	1.14	17.3	.273	.602

[1] *Pext* (%) = percentage who responded with the most extreme response choice

except for number of sports teams. For each group of items (i.e., school, risk, health), we then counted the number of items scored in the extreme for each youth. Conducting independent samples t-tests revealed that numbers of youths scoring in the extreme range was significantly different between samples for all groups of items. Target youths had a significantly higher number of extreme responses on school items ($M = .7391$, $SD = 1.4378$, range = 0 to 7) than the comparison group ($M = .04589$, $SD = .2515$, range = 0 to 3), $t(826) = 9.663$, $p = .001$. Only 4% of youths in the comparison group had any extreme responses to school items as compared to 34% of youths in the target group. Of the target youths, 6 responded to the extreme response on every item. Target youths also had a significantly higher number of extreme responses on risk items ($M = .4155$, $SD = 1.1270$, range = 0 to 5) than the comparison group ($M = .03623$, $SD = .2531$, range = 0 to 3), $t(826) = 6.680$, $p = .000$. Only

3% of the comparison group had any extreme responses to risk items as compared to 18% of target youths. Of the target youths, 16 responded to the extreme response on every item. Finally, target youths had a significantly higher number of extreme responses on health items ($M = .6812$, $SD = .8965$, range = 0 to 4) than the comparison group ($M = .4928$, $SD = .8078$, range = 0 to 4), $t(826) = 3.177$, $p = .002$. Whereas 34% of youths in the comparison group had any extreme responses to health items, 46% of target youths had extreme responses to health items. In addition, 6 target youths and 2 comparison group youths had extreme responses to all four health items.

DISCUSSION

There is extremely limited information about the psychometric characteristics of the school violence, risk and health items embedded within the YRBS. The Centers for Disease Control undertakes a significant effort every other year to gather high-quality information about the incidence of youth health risk and promotion behaviors. The YRBS has had significant, positive influences on researchers and public policy (e.g., U.S. Surgeon General, 2000). School violence research has also specifically benefited from the information gleaned from the YRBS initiative (DeVoe et al., 2002; U.S. Departments of Education and Justice, 2000). Despite this prominent position in school violence research, there is limited empirical investigation of the YRBS's reliability and validity. In this article, we examined one aspect of the response validity using a small subset of youths in the 2001 YRBS sample (3%) who indicated that they had carried a weapon to school 6 or more times in the past 30 days. Certainly some of these youths accurately reported their behavior, and such frequent school weapon possession is a serious matter of concern. However, given YRBS data-editing procedures, it is possible that such frequent self-reported school weapon possession could be due to other factors. One such alternate explanation was supported by the results of the current study—some of these youths had a response pattern such that they were more likely to select the most extreme response option. Cornell and Loeper (1998) also found this response pattern in a previous study using a regional school safety survey.

Results indicated that those youths who reported they carried a gun to school 6 or more times in the past 30 days were significantly more likely to give the most extreme response to other school safety and risk behaviors than a matched comparison group. To the extent that cases with such response patterns are included in the YRBS sample, the estimate of school risk prevalence will be inflated. We note that the YRBS extreme response options can describe very unusual behaviors, particularly when considered in the context of a student being reliable enough to be at school on the day of the survey and lucid enough to respond to the survey. For example, 6.2% of the extreme gun response group indicated that they had alcohol on school property *all 30 days* in the past month (this, of course, requires the student to consume alcohol every Saturday and Sunday at school, a seemingly very unlikely behavior), and 10.8% indicated that they had used marijuana *40 or more times* at school in the past 30 days. In addition, 5.3% of the 414 youths in the extreme school weapon group indicated that they had engaged in both extreme rates of school alcohol and marijuana use in the previous month. Clearly, such a response pattern is implausible. Nonetheless, such extreme risk behaviors certainly speak to very high–risk behaviors and would be a matter of intense concern. However, additional analyses indicated that the extreme school weapon group was more likely than the comparison youth to drink 4 or more glasses of milk per day, to eat carrots 4 or more times per day, and 32.8% indicated that they engaged in daily aerobic exercise during the previous week. Furthermore, 3.9% of the extreme school weapon group gave the most extreme response to all 5 of the substance use risk items–this means that in the past 30 days they had binged on alcohol on 20 or more days and inhaled substances 40 or more times, and in their lifetime had taken heroin and steroids 40 or more times. These same youths also had attempted suicide 6 or more times in the previous year. Such a pattern of intense risk behaviors would be debilitating and preclude valid participation in a school-wide survey such as the YRBS. There are multiple reasons why these students may respond in the extreme, such as a cry for help, exaggerating symptoms as suggested by Rogers et al. (2002) or merely filling in bubbles on the right side of the form. Thus, a data-cleaning process would help to take into account extreme responders.

    Although this exploratory study examined a small subset of youths, it is crucial because research has increasingly focused on risk patterns involving rare school violence events. In this case, weapons carrying may be a risk factor that is directly related to violent offenses on school campuses, and as such is worthy of careful examination. As this study illustrates, the response patterns of this subset must be examined carefully, as the YRBS does not have a screening mechanism for those who respond in the extreme to such questions. For example, though many of these youths may have reported honestly about their extreme behavior, studies have shown that there is a subset of youths who do respond in the extreme as a form of defiance to authority (Rogers et al., 2002).

Critique of the YRBS: School Safety Item Reliability

In addition to examining the case-wise validity of the YRBS responses, there are as yet unsettled questions about its reliability. In their analysis of the reliability of the 1999 YRBS, Brener et al. (2002) concluded that

> . . . any inconsistent response in this study was considered to be a response error when calculating kappa. It is possible, however, that an inconsistent response between Time 1 and Time 2 could reflect an actual behavior change. For example, a student could report at Time 1 that he had not smoked cigarettes in the past 30 days, then report at Time 2 that he had smoked in the past 30 days. Such responses would be inconsistent yet accurate if the student did indeed smoke during the 2-week test-retest interval and not before. The values of kappa computed for this study, therefore, must be considered to be conservative estimates. (p. 341)

Although such changes in short-term behaviors should be accurately measured by the YRBS, the methodology used by Brener et al. (2002) appears to have optimized the kappa values. For example, they also found that the ". . . mean kappas were somewhat higher for questions that used lifetime as a reference period than those that used the past 30 days and the past 12 months, these differences were not statistically significant" (p. 340). This, however, would appear to be problematic. It should be anticipated that given the two-week test-retest time period, items with a 30-day time frame (50% of the referent time) should have shown more change than the items with a past year (3.8% of the referent time) response period. In fact, the two-week time period, for this test-retest was inappropriate for the past year and lifetime items. None of the school safety and only one related school behavior item (had an HIV class) has a lifetime time reference, *which has the lowest kappa of all YRBS items*. Of the four items that ask directly about school safety matters, two (fighting and threatened) items use a 12-month reference and two use a past 30-day referent. None of these items have markedly substantial kappas, and the stability of the 12-month items never exceeds the 30-day items.

The methodology used in the Brener et al. (2002) YRBS stability analysis reduced the amount of discrepancy between responses in two ways. First, data editing screened for inconsistent responses and recoded these values as missing for both responses. These cases, by definition, provided inconsistent or unreliable responses, and this source of error was removed from these calculations. Second, in converting all items to binary values any other inconsistencies in the frequency of responses (e.g., a youth indicating that they had been in a fight at school six or more times in the past year at Time 1 and then two weeks later indicating that they had been in only one fight in the past year) were ignored. Thus, the methods used to estimate the consistencies of youth responses provide the *best* estimates of reliability. Even with this approach, kappas for the school items were marginally acceptable at best. Given that the focus of the primary YRBS analysis is to provide population estimates, this approach is perhaps understandable. There is currently no reliability information about using the YRBS to combine items into scales or attempt to examine more precise frequency rates. A particular concern with respect to the YRBS school safety items is that safety perception and threat items do not appear to have adequate two-week response consistency even when recoded as a binary response. The items concerning school fights and weapon carrying are better, but not markedly so.

The reliability of the YRBS school safety items is a critical matter because researchers continue to use the YRBS data in a manner that assumes its scores have known stability over time. For example, in one important study, Brener, Simon, Anderson, Barrios, and Small (2002) sought to examine the effects of the shootings at Columbine High School on reports of violence-related behaviors. Data collected for the 1999 YRBS were used and compared with data collected before and after the April 20, 1999, shootings. They reported that students who completed YRBS post-Columbine were more likely to report that they felt unsafe to go to school one or more of the 30 days before the survey (10.2% vs. 3.9% pre-Columbine). Interestingly, the post-Columbine responders were significantly less likely to report considering suicide or making a suicide plan than the pre-Columbine group. Of interest is that this is one of the few studies that have examined the possible sensitivity of the YRBS to such a dramatic historical event. However, the methodology used divided the 1999 national sample by the date of the Columbine event and did not consider the manner in which each item's time frames fit with the study's objectives. For example, a student who completed the YRBS one week after Columbine was asked to comment on lifetime, past year, and 30-day behaviors, almost all of which would had occurred *prior to* the Columbine incident. The results suggest that the YRBS may be sensitive to historical influences, but that this is not necessarily a good methodological outcome because it raises questions about the students' ability to accurately recall previous events. To provide lasting utility as a surveillance tool, YRBS items need to demonstrate greater long-term stability and less sensitivity to near-term historical events. The marginal kappas suggest that youths do not respond consistently over even short periods of time (14 days) and thus raises questions about accuracy of the behaviors measured by the YRBS.

CONCLUSION

Though originally developed for epidemiological research, behavioral researchers have increasingly used the YRBS in order to examine characteristics of youths who engage in risky behavior (e.g., evaluation; Doniger, Adams, Utter, & Riley, 2001). However, the YRBS data have not been carefully screened for this purpose. When completing item-by-item analyses with information dichotomized from the original response choices, extreme responding would have only a minimal effect on results. However, when used to understand those youths who respond in the extreme, a thoughtful examination is warranted and case-wise data screening is necessary. Secondary analyses of the YRBS should regularly report information about how missing information was managed; this is not now common practice.

A key question involving any survey such as the YRBS is: What level of precision is needed for its purposes and are researchers willing to accept? Given the high visibility of YRBS survey results and their impact on research and public policy, we argue that it ought to be held to the highest standards of psychometric rigor. If the goal of the YRBS is to estimate population parameters, it may now meet this criterion, although with respect to school violence research the performance of the school-based items requires more scrutiny. However, over the years, the YRBS's roles have increasingly expanded to examine individual differences and to assess the correlates of health risk behaviors. Such applications can be based only on an instrument with carefully documented psychometric characteristics. For this reason, we conclude that future YRBS analyses could easily include (a) validity check items that assess the validity of student responses such as suggested by Rosenblatt and Furlong (1997); (b) global veracity items such as those suggested by Cornell and Loeper (1998); (c) compliance responses such as directions to fill in a certain response option; and (d) the coding of all public access YRBS files with information about nonresponses versus inconsistent responses.

NOTES

1. The mean number of items coded as missing for a youth in the 2001 YRBS data set is 4.21 (SD = 7.83), with a range from 0 to 71 items missing out of a possible 95. Less then half of the sample had no missing data (48.8%). In addition, 46.6% had two or more missing responses, 10% had 13 or more missing responses, and 5% had 22 or more missing responses.

2. We also note that there were five school behavior items that had parallel items that did not specify any particular setting (e.g., being in a physical fight in the past 12 months). For all these items, the school item presumably represented a subset of the behaviors captured by its parallel item. Thus, the prevalence rates would be lower, but there is no reason to believe that the response consistency would be different. For all five of these items, the school setting items had lower kappa by an average of 10.0.

REFERENCES

Becher, J. C., Garcia, J. G., Kaplan, D. W., Gil, A. R., Li, J., Main, D., Herrera, J. A., Arias, L., & Bromet, A. (1999). Reproduction health risk behavior survey of Columbian high school Students. *Journal of Adolescent Health, 24*(3), 220-225.

Brener, N. D., Collins, J. L., Kann, L., Warren, C. W., & Williams, B. I. (1995). Reliability of the youth risk behavior surveillance system questionnaire. *American Journal of Epidemiology, 141,* 575-580.

Brener, N. D., Kann, L., McManus, T., Kinchen, S. A., Sundberg, E. C., & Ross, J. G. (2002). Reliability of the 1999 Youth Risk Behavior Survey Questionnaire. *Journal of Adolescent Health, 31,* 336-342.

Brener, N. D., Simon, T., Anderson, M., Barrios, L. C., & Small, M. L. (2002). Effect of the incident at Columbine on students' violence- and suicide-related behaviors. *American Journal of Preventative Medicine, 22,* 146-150.

Cleary, S. D. (2000). Adolescent victimization and associated suicidal and violent behaviors. *Adolescence, 35,* 671-682.

Coggeshall, M. B., & Kingery, P. M. (2001). Cross-survey analysis of school violence and disorder. *Psychology in the Schools, 38,* 107-116.

Cornell, D. G., & Loeper, A. B. (1998). Assessment of violence and other high-risk behaviors with a school survey. *School Psychology Review, 27*(2), 317-330.

DeVoe, J. F., Peter, K., Kaufman, P., Ruddy, S. A., Miller, A. K., Planty, M., Snyder, T. D., Duhart, D. T., & Rand, M. R. (2002). *Indicators of school crime and safety: 2002.* Washington, DC: U.S. Departments of Education and Justice. NCES 2003-009/NCJ196753.

Doniger, A. S., Adams, E., Utter, C. A., & Riley, J. S. (2001). Impact evaluation of the "Not Me, Not Now" abstinence-oriented, adolescent pregnancy prevention communications program, Monroe County, New York. *Journal of Health Communication, 6*(1), 45-60.

DuRant, R. H., Rickert, V. I., Ashworth, C. S., Newman, C. et al. (1993). The association of sexual risk behaviors and problem drug behaviors in high school students. *New England Journal of Medicine, 328*(13), 922-926.

Everett, S. A., Giovino, G. A., Warren, C. W., Crossett, L., & Kann, L. (1998). Other substance use among high school students who use tobacco. *Journal of Adolescent Health, 23*(5), 289-296.

Faulkner, A. H., & Cranston, K. (1998). Correlates of same-sex sexual behavior in a random sample of Massachusetts's high school students. *American Journal of Public Health, 88*(2), 262-266.

Felts, W. M., Parrillo, A. V., Chenier, T., & Dunn, P. (1996). Adolescents' perceptions of relative weight and self-reported weight-loss activities: Analysis of 1990 YRBS national data. *Journal of Adolescent Health, 18*(1), 20-26.

Furlong, M. J., Bates, M. P., Sharkey, J. D., & Smith, D. C. (2004). The accuracy of school and non-school risk behaviors as predictors of school weapons possession. In M. J. Furlong, M. P. Bates, D. C. Smith, & P. E. Kingery (Eds.), *Appraisal and prediction of school violence: Methods, issues, and contexts.* Hauppauge, NY: NovaScience Publishers.

Furlong, M. J., Bates, M. P., & Smith, D. C. (2001). Predicting school weapon possession: A secondary analysis of the Youth Risk Behavior Surveillance Survey. *Psychology in the Schools, 38,* 127-139.

Garry, J. P., Morrissey, S. L., & Whetstone, L. M. (2003). Substance use and weight loss tactics among middle school youth. *International Journal of Eating Disorders, 33*(1), 55-63.

Grunbaum, J., Lowry, R., & Kann, L. (2001). Prevalence of health-related behaviors among alternative high school students as compared with students attending regular high schools. *Journal of Adolescent Health, 29*(5), 337-343.

Grunbaum, J., Lowry, R., Kann, L., & Pateman, B. (2000). Focus on Asian American/Pacific Islander student risk behaviors. *Journal of Adolescent Health, 27*(5), 322-330.

Gwede, C. K., McDermott, R. J., Westhoff, W. W., Mushore, M., Mushore, T., Chitsika, E., Majange, C. S., & Chauke, P. (2001). Health risk behavior of rural secondary school students in Zimbabwe. *Health Education & Behavior, 29*(5), 608-623.

Hennessy, M. (1999). Adolescent syndromes of risk for HIV infection. *Evaluation Review, 18*(3), 312-341.

Hill, S. C. (1998). School-related violence: A secondary analysis of the Youth Risk Behavior Survey data. *Dissertation Abstracts International Section A: Humanities & Social Sciences, 58*(9-A), 3434.

Hou, S., & Basen-Engquist, K. (1997). Human immunodeficiency virus risk behavior among White and Asian/Pacific Islander high school students in the United States: Does culture make a difference? *Journal of Adolescent Health, 20*(1), 68-74.

Klein, J. D., Graff, C. A., Santelli, J. S., Allan, M. J., & Elster, A. B. (2001). Improving adolescent health care surveillance. In M. A. Cynamon & R. A. Kulka (Eds.), *Seventh conference on health survey research methods* (pp. 11-18). DHHS Pub No. 01-1013. Hyattsville, MD: National Center for Health Statistics.

Kolbe L. J., Kann L., & Collins, J. L. (1993). Overview of the Youth Risk Behavior Surveillance System. *Public Health Rep, 108*(Suppl 1), 2-10.

Light, H. (1998). Sex differences in adolescent high-risk sexual and drug behaviors. *Psychological Reports, 82*(3, Pt 2),1312-1314.

Lowry, R., Powell, K. E., Kann, L., Collins, J. L., & Kolbe, L. J. (1998). Weapon-carrying, physical fighting, and fight-related injury among U.S. adolescents. *American Journal of Preventive Medicine, 14*(2), 122-129.

Luke, D. A., Stamatakis, K. A., & Brownson, R. C. (2000). State youth-access tobacco control policies and youth smoking behavior in the United States. *American Journal of Preventive Medicine, 19*(3), 180-187.

Maclure, M., & Willett, W. C. (1987). Misinterpretation and misuse of the kappa statistic. *American Journal of Epidemiology, 126,* 161-169.

Melnick, M. J., Miller, K. E., Sabo, D. F., Farrell, M. P., & Barnes, G. M. (2001). Tobacco use among high school athletes and nonathletes: Results of the 1997 Youth Risk Behavior Survey. *Adolescence, 36*(144), 727-747.

Merrill, J. C., Kleber, H. D., Shwartz, M., Liu, H., & Lewis, S. R. (1999). Cigarettes, alcohol, marijuana, other risk behaviors, and American youth. *Drug & Alcohol Dependence, 56*(3), 205-212.

Miller, K. E., Barnes, G. M., Sabo, D., Melnick, M. J., & Farrell, M. P. (2002). A comparison of health risk behavior in adolescent users of anabolic-androgenic steroids, by gender and athlete status. *Sociology of Sport Journal, 19*(4), 385-402.

Nelson, D. E., Moon, R. W., Holtzman, D., Smith, P., & Siegel, P. Z. (1997). Patterns of health risk behaviors for chronic disease: A comparison between adolescent and adult American Indians living on or near reservations in Montana. *Adolescent Health, 21,* 25-32.

Orpinas, P. K., Basen-Engquist, K., Grunbaum, J., & Parcel, G. S. (1995). The co-morbidity of violence-related behaviors with health-risk behaviors in a population of high school students. *Journal of Adolescent Health, 16*(3), 216-225.

Page, R. M., & Zarco, E. P. (2001). Shyness, physical activity, and sports team participation among Philippine high school students. *Child Study Journal, 31*(3), 193-204.

Pesa, J. A., & Turner, L. W. (2001). Fruit and vegetables intake and weight-control behaviors among U.S. youth. *American Journal of Health Behavior, 25*(1), 3-9.

Pierre, N., Shrier, L. A., Emans, S. J., & DuRant, R. H. (1998). Adolescent males involved in pregnancy: Associations of forced sexual contact and risk behaviors. *Journal of Adolescent Health, 23*(6), 364-369.

Rogers, R., Vitacco, M. J., Jackson, R. L., Martin, M., Collins, M., & Sewell, K. W. (2002). Faking psychopathology? An examination of response styles with antisocial youth. *Journal of Personality Assessment, 78,* 31-46.

Rosenblatt, J. A., & Furlong, M. J. (1997). Assessing the reliability and validity of student self-reports of campus violence. *Journal of Youth and Adolescence, 26,* 187-202.

Shrier, L. A., Emans, S. J., Woods, E. R., & DuRant, R. H. (1997). The association of sexual risk behaviors and problem drug behaviors in high school students. *Journal of Adolescent Health, 20*(5), 377-383.

U.S. Departments of Education and Justice. (2000). *2000 annual report on school safety.* Washington, DC: Author.

U.S. Surgeon General. (2000). *Youth violence: A report of the U.S. Surgeon General.* Retrieved, July 17, 2003, from http://www.mentalhealth.org/youthviolence/surgeongeneral/SG_Site/summary.asp

Valois, R. F., Bryant, E. S., Rivard, J. C., & Hinkle, K. T. (1997). Sexual risk-taking behaviors among adolescents with severe emotional disturbance. *Journal of Child & Family Studies*, 6(4), 409-419.

Valois, R. F., Dunham, A. C. A., Jackson, K. L., & Waller, J. (1999). Association between employment and substance abuse behaviors among public high school adolescents. *Journal of Adolescent Health*, 25(4), 256-263.

APPENDIX A

2001 Youth Risk Behavior Surveillance Survey Items Included in Analyses

Item	Question	Extreme Response	Group
15	During the past 30 days, on how many days did you carry a weapon such as a gun, knife, or club on school property?	6 or more days	Target
16	During the past 30 days, on how many days did you not go to school because you felt you would be unsafe at school or on your way to or from school?	6 or more days	School
17	During the past 12 months, how many times has someone threatened or injured you with a weapon such as a gun, knife, or club on school property?	12 or more times	School
20	During the past 12 months, how many times were you in a physical fight on school property?	12 or more times	School
34	During the past 30 days, on how many days did you smoke cigarettes on school property?	All 30 days	School
38	During the past 30 days, on how many days did you use chewing tobacco, snuff, or dip on school property?	All 30 days	School
44	During the past 30 days, on how many days did you have at least one drink of alcohol on school property?	All 30 days	School
48	During the past 30 days, how many times did you use marijuana on school property?	40 or more times	School
26	During the past 12 months, how many times did you actually attempt suicide?	6 or more times	Risk
43	During the past 30 days, on how many days did you have 5 or more drinks of alcohol in a row, that is, within a couple of hours?	20 or more days	Risk
52	During the past 30 days, how many times have you sniffed glue, breathed the contents of aerosol spray cans, or inhaled any paints or sprays to get high?	40 or more times	Risk
53	During your life, how many times have you used heroin (also called smack, junk, or China White)?	40 or more times	Risk
55	During your life, how many times have you taken steroid pills or shots without a doctor's prescription?	40 or more times	Risk
77	During the past 7 days, how many times did you eat carrots?	4 or more times per day	Health
79	During the past 7 days, how many glasses of milk did you drink?	4 or more glasses per day	Health
80	On how many of the past 7 days did you exercise or participate in physical activity for at least 20 minutes that made you sweat and breathe hard, such as basketball, soccer, running, swimming laps, fast bicycling, fast dancing, or similar aerobic activities?	7 days	Health
86	During the past 12 months, on how many sports teams did you play?	3 or more teams	Health

Structural Equation Modeling of School Violence Data: Methodological Considerations

Matthew J. Mayer

SUMMARY. Methodological challenges associated with structural equation modeling (SEM) and structured means modeling (SMM) in research on school violence and related topics in the social and behavioral sciences are examined. Problems associated with multiyear implementations of large-scale surveys are discussed. Complex sample designs, part of any large-scale survey, introduce multiple methodological challenges into SEM analysis. Problems with missing data and data imputation procedures are explored, along with commonly occurring departures from normality. Hypothesis testing of models and associated fit indices are explicated. Issues surrounding the use of Lagrange Multiplier tests of constraint validity in SMM are examined. Finally, basic problems asso-

---

Dr. Matthew J. Mayer directs the Special Education Program in Emotional Impairment at Michigan State University. Dr. Mayer is currently the national secretary of the Council for Children with Behavioral Disorders and is also a resource fellow for the National Center on Education, Disability, and Juvenile Justice (EDJJ). His research interests include school violence and disruption, technology-based instruction for students with emotional/behavioral disorders, positive behavioral supports in special education, discipline issues in special education, and special education law.

Address correspondence to: Dr. Matthew J. Mayer, Erickson Hall Room 340, Michigan State University, East Lansing, MI 48824 (E-mail: mayerma@msu.edu).

[Haworth co-indexing entry note]: "Structural Equation Modeling of School Violence Data: Methodological Considerations." Mayer, Matthew J. Co-published simultaneously in *Journal of School Violence* (The Haworth Press, Inc.) Vol. 3, No. 2/3, 2004, pp. 131-148; and: *Issues in School Violence Research* (ed: Michael J. Furlong et al.) The Haworth Press, Inc., 2004, pp. 131-148. Single or multiple copies of this article are available for a fee from The Haworth Document Delivery Service [1-800-HAWORTH, 9:00 a.m. - 5:00 p.m. (EST). E-mail address: docdelivery@haworthpress.com].

http://www.haworthpress.com/web/JSV
© 2004 by The Haworth Press, Inc. All rights reserved.
Digital Object Identifier: 10.1300/J202v03n02_08

ciated with developing viable models of complex social phenomena with SEM are considered. *[Article copies available for a fee from The Haworth Document Delivery Service: 1-800-HAWORTH. E-mail address: <docdelivery@haworthpress.com> Website: <http://www.HaworthPress.com> © 2004 by The Haworth Press, Inc. All rights reserved.]*

KEYWORDS. Surveys, school violence, methodological, Lagrange Multiplier tests, structural equation modeling

Structural equation modeling (SEM) is a technique that has gained popularity in the social and behavioral sciences since the early 1980s. SEM uses maximum likelihood and related iterative techniques for concurrent solution of regression equations that depict directional relationships among model factors, based on fitting data to a covariance model. SEM allows researchers to model structural relationships among posited latent variables that cannot be measured directly, but for which adequate indirect measurements exist. SEM grew out of regression and factor analysis, but represents a more powerful approach than simple linear regression, ANOVA, path analysis, or factor analysis. Structural equation modeling is more a confirmatory method, as opposed to exploratory, and has been successfully used to facilitate understanding of complex processes in fields as diverse as education, psychology, political theory, economics, and medicine. While SEM provides hypothesis testing of models, causal determinations linked to fitted models must be tempered with knowledge of inherent limitations of the method (Cliff, 1983; Hoyle & Smith, 1994). Evidence to support causal hypotheses based on SEM analyses can be particularly compelling when tested with nested models. SEM methods do not provide an absolute test of causality (Hoyle, 1995). "A model is disconfirmable to the degree that it is possible for the model to be inconsistent with observed data" (MacCallum, 1995).

Research on school violence often seeks to explicate processes associated with violence and disruption as well as related causal influences. Several researchers have used these techniques to identify key variables associated with school violence and disruption (Gottfredson & Gottfredson, 1985; Karcher, 2002; Mandell, Hill, Carter, & Brandon, 2002; Mayer, 2001; Mayer & Leone, 1999). For example, Mayer and Leone (1999) and Mayer (2001) examined a model explaining the contributions of secure building strategies and systems of law to school violence. Karcher investigated a model for the cycle of violence and disconnectedness among rural students (see Figure 1). Researchers with

FIGURE 1. Karcher (2002) SEM diagram.

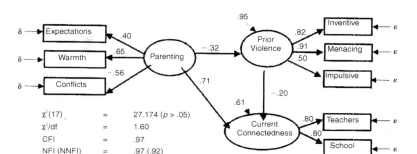

This figure was originally published in Karcher, M. J. (2002). The cycle of violence and disconnection among rural middle school students: Teacher disconnection as a consequence of violence. *Journal of School Violence*, *1*(1), 45. © by The Haworth Press, Inc.

the Washington Kids Count Project (Mandell et al., 2002) modeled the connections among substance abuse, violent and delinquent behaviors, and academic achievement. Similar research has been conducted examining individual, peer, family, and school-related factors connected to school violence and disruption.

The purpose of this article is to examine a number of methodological challenges researchers face while performing structural equation modeling and structured means modeling (SMM) in research on school violence and related topics in the social and behavioral sciences. This article begins with a brief conceptual overview of SEM and SMM methods. Next, data sources to support SEM and SMM research are considered, with particular attention to a prominent national dataset, the School Crime Supplement to the National Crime Victimization Survey. Fundamental issues pertaining to the measurement model and associated issues with datasets will be examined. Multiyear implementations of large-scale surveys with instrumentation revisions will be discussed. Complex sample designs, part of any large-scale survey, introduce multiple methodological challenges into SEM analysis. The SEM literature has begun to address these issues in recent years. Problems with missing data and data imputation procedures will be explored, along with the commonly occurring departures from normality. Hypothesis testing with chi-square, which is sensitive to large sample size, will be considered, along with a brief discussion of fit indices and trade-offs and general procedures for selecting and using these measures of model fit. Problems associated with ordered categorical variables are discussed. Issues surrounding the use of Lagrange Multiplier tests of constraint validity in SMM will be explored. Finally, the basic problems associated with developing viable interpretations for modeling complex social phenomena through SEM will be considered. Each of the topical components of this article could easily warrant an entire journal article or book chapter. The basic issues will be identified and discussed in each area, with the reader referred to more detailed sources for further study.

OVERVIEW OF STRUCTURAL EQUATION MODELING AND STRUCTURED MEANS MODELING

Structural equation modeling uses covariance matrix analysis to compare the fit between an implied covariance matrix (model-based) and the observed (sample) matrix based on the investigator's data. While confirmatory in nature, SEM typically takes on one of three approaches: (a) strictly confirmatory, (b) alternative model fitting, and (c) model development. Cross-validation procedures are typically used in the latter case (Hoyle, 1995). SEM may be considered in terms of the measurement model and the structural model. The measurement model represents the hypothesized loading of the latent factors on the measured (*manifest*) variables, commonly considered as a confirmatory factor analysis (CFA) model. The structural model posits directional linkages among latent variables. In SEM diagrams, latent variables are normally represented by circles or ellipses, and observed variables are represented by rectangles (see Figure 1). SEM diagrams also explicitly model error (*disturbance*) terms linked to specific measured variables and endogenous latent factors.

While models can be tested using a chi-square procedure, specific fit indices (discussed further below) are used to evaluate model fit. Chi-square-based testing is more compelling when carried out within a nested model system. In nested models, the numbers of parameters that are free to be estimated in one variation of the model are a subset of another part of the system. Model testing within a nested system generally seeks the most parsimonious explanation of the data demonstrating the strongest fit. Models are typically studied using standardized path coefficients to facilitate easy comparison. SEM uses a two-step procedure, where initially, the measurement model is developed, using a "perfect" structural model (all latent factors are allowed to covary). Finally, the structural model is reimposed and evaluated, using appropriate fit indices.

Structured Means Modeling (SMM) maps the means of measured variables onto their respective latent means. In SMM, researchers model variances, covariances, and means simultaneously. Parameters associated with the data-based distributions that are compared are constrained so that a relative difference between the latent means can be assessed (see Figure 2). There is no absolute scale of measurement when comparing latent means. The resultant change is measured in *effect size*, reported in standard deviation units (Hancock, 2001). The researcher can "force" two distributions under comparison to sit on the same conceptual line (see Figure 3), and compare their means by (a) constraining

FIGURE 2. Structured means model.

N.B.: Path set to zero to allow means comparison
N.B.: Path is estimated
Group 1
Group 2
V999
LV 1
D1*
MV1
MV2
MV3
E1*
N.B.: Paths with same letter preceded by * are estimated but constrained equal across groups
The paths from LV1 to MV1 are set = 1 for scale determination purposes (could be MV2 or MV3 instead)

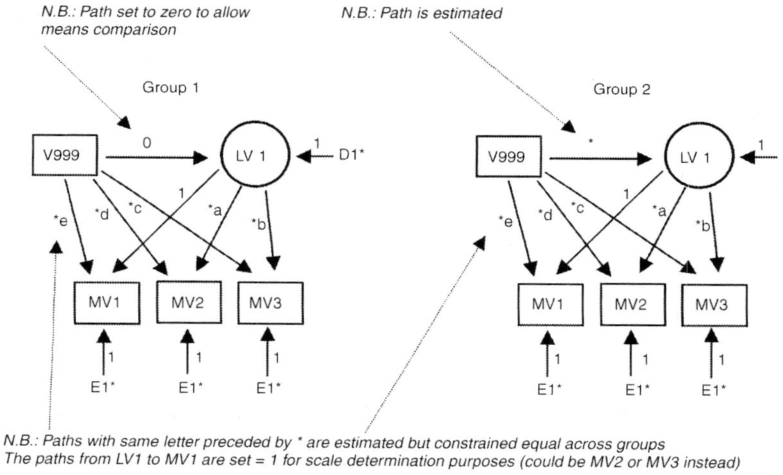

FIGURE 3. Distributions for comparison of means in SMM.

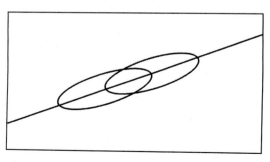

paths ("slopes") from latent variables (L.V.s) to their respective measured variables (M.V.s) to be equal across groups being compared for changes in latent means; and (b) constraining paths ("intercepts") from the V999 (in the EQS software) constant pseudovariable (a column of 1s) to the measured variables to be equal across groups.

WORKING WITH NATIONAL DATASETS

Analysis of processes associated with school violence and disruption can require access to a large-scale dataset such as the School Crime Supplement (SCS) to the National Crime Victimization Survey (NCVS). While researchers are free to construct and use their own instrumentation, pursuing such efforts on a national scale can be cost prohibitive. In turn, this discussion will explore issues associated with using the SCS and similar existing national datasets for SEM analysis. Using data collected for other research purposes naturally constrains the scope of investigation to align with the survey instrument questions and associated variables in the public access dataset. Common problems can include (a) limited number of indicator variables, (b) measurement scale and range issues, (c) changes in questionnaire instruments across years, and (d) changes in response codes across years.

Mayer and Leone (1999) and Mayer (2001) modeled the relationship among secure building strategies and systems of law to school violence (see Figure 4). Three of the four latent variables are each associated with only two measured variables. This illustrates a common limitation in using national datasets in that they may, at best, partially align with specific model development goals due to the limited number of useful indicator variables. In this case, the measured variables used by Mayer and Leone were composite (derived) variables, built through combining the responses on multiple questionnaire items. Although it is generally recommended that at least three indicator variables accompany each latent variable (Bentler & Chou, 1987; Hoyle & Smith, 1994), this was not feasible in this analysis. With three or more measured variables per latent construct, and a very high degree of fit, the likelihood of plausible alternative models with a very high degree of fit is relatively small. Conversely, with only two measured variables for a latent construct (as in this research), the likelihood of alternative plausible models is greatly increased. Hence, SEM model development that depends on the convenient availability of existing large datasets may be limited in its ability to adequately depict social processes

FIGURE 4. Mayer (2001) SEM analysis.

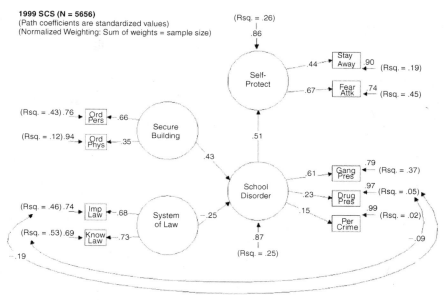

1999 SCS (N = 5656)
(Path coefficients are standardized values)
(Normalized Weighting: Sum of weights = sample size)

Robust CFI = .964

because a limited number of indicator variables can greatly increase the likely existence of plausible competing models.

Another common problem associated with using external (to the researcher) datasets for SEM research relates to the range of measured variable values and, related to that, the presence of ordered categorical variables (discussed further below). A few of the measured variables described above have scores with a range of 0-3, representing ordered categorical variables, while others had vastly different value ranges. Due to basic mathematical principles of matrix algebra, large differences in scales of input variables can lead to wild differences in the variance of the respective variables, which in turn can cause problems obtaining solutions to covariance matrices (they are hard to manipulate and difficult to invert–a prerequisite to obtaining a solution). Accordingly, Bentler (1995) suggested that input variables be purposefully scaled so as to force roughly similar variances.

Questionnaire consistency can be particularly problematic while working with multiyear implementations of national surveys. For example, the 1995 and 1999 SCS questionnaires are not identical. Some wording changes occurred in a few questions between the two versions of the surveys. An example of a change in wording follows. In the 1995 SCS questionnaire, item 15 reads, "Does your school take any particular measures to ensure the safety of students? For example, does the school have: (a) Security guards? (b) Other school staff supervising the hallway? (c) Metal detectors? (d) Locked doors during the day? (e) A requirement that visitors sign in? (f) Locker checks?" In the 1999 version, the same question reads, "Does your school take any particular measures to ensure the safety of students? For example, does the school have: (a) Security guards *and/or assigned police officers*? (b) Other school staff *or other adults* supervising the hallway? (c) Metal detectors? (d) Locked *entrance or exit* doors during the day? (e) A requirement that visitors sign in? (f) Locker checks?"

Subparts (a), (b), and (d) changed somewhat between the 1995 and 1999 questionnaires. It is unclear whether students in the 1999 survey would have answered subpart (a) in the same manner had the wording not included "and/or assigned police officers." Likewise, the addition of the words, "or other adults" in subpart (b) changes the meaning slightly. The explicit mention of "entrance or exit doors" in subpart (d) also makes the 1999 version of the question different. Similar difficulties existed due to wording changes in other questions, such as those pertaining to the availability of drugs in school. Researchers working with multiyear surveys must be extremely attentive to and take extra caution with regard to changes in questionnaire wording.

Another problem resulting from changes in instrumentation from year to year relates to variable coding. The coding of the responses to certain victimization questions differed between the 1995 and 1999 SCS questionnaires due to screener questions used in the 1999 SCS questionnaire. In order to make the coding comparable, the researcher (Mayer, 2001) had to address "out of universe" codes in the 1999 SCS victimization questions that resulted from respondents answering "no" to both screener questions. The "out of universe" codes were recoded to values representing a response of "no," thus making the 1995 and 1999 variable codes compatible for analysis purposes. Researchers performing SEM research on multiyear survey data must perform side-by-side analysis of dataset codebooks (from different survey administrations) to identify and address any changes in variable coding. While any dataset can present challenges associated with measurement scales, the issues associated with ordered categorical variables in SEM research can be problematic when working with external datasets.

ORDERED CATEGORICAL VARIABLES

Ordered categorical variables (e.g., "low-medium-high" responses) can present difficulty because they are not necessarily tied to the continuous distribution theory upon which many analytic procedures are based. Coarsely categorical data can be analyzed using appropriate specifications to the software, identifying categorical variables, including ordered categorical variables with, say, two to four categories. However, special procedures to handle this scenario, such as the "categories" procedure in EQS, or Muthen's CVS, or continuous/categorical variable methodology (West, Finch, & Curran, 1995), assume that these coarsely categorized variables are tied to an underlying continuous distribution. Such an assumption may not be warranted. On the other hand, in cases where coarsely categorized variables have four or more levels, they can be treated as if they have an underlying continuous distribution (Bentler & Chou, 1987; West et al., 1995) using traditional robust estimation methods that have been shown to provide adequate results with such variables. Additionally, problems can exist with non-normality of data associated with dichotomous and coarsely categorized variables (Kaplan, 2000), and SEM researchers have often failed to address normal theory assumptions tied to their research (West et al., 1995).

The problems relating to ordered categorical variables and other topics mentioned above can pose serious problems for the researcher and must be addressed in a systematic and rigorous manner. Corrective procedures are available in most circumstances. In addition to these basic problems, most large-scale regional and national surveys employ complex sample designs, introducing other methodological challenges.

COMPLEX SAMPLE DESIGNS

Most large-scale surveys use complex sample designs that typically involve some combination of two or more of the following: (a) cluster sampling, (b) stratification of clusters and elements within clusters, and (c) weights resulting from unequal but known selection probabilities. Simple random sampling is rarely performed. Complex survey designs are known to produce sampling variances for estimates that are larger than those for simple random samples of the same size (Kish, 1965). Use of standard statistical software, which employs estimation procedures based on simple random sampling, can result in underestimation of standard errors and incorrect inference-based decisions based on the results of significance tests. In the context of SEM, the effect of the complex sample design on estimated standard errors of path coefficients is known to be smaller than the effect on other statistics (Kish & Frankel, 1974). In the past, SEM analysis software has estimated standard errors under such assumptions, and typically has had no features to take the sample design into account in estimated standard errors. It is possible to compensate by revised estimation of standard errors using bootstrap or jackknife procedures. However, those procedures require special programming to implement. Several recent versions of leading SEM software have begun to address this issue, allowing researchers to input weighting variables as well as data on clustering and stratification.

Recent SEM methodological research has focused on complex sample design issues (Kaplan & Ferguson, 1999; Muthen & Satorra, 1995). Muthen and Satorra used Monte Carlo methods on a simulated national level survey with a complex sample design. They demonstrated a robust-type procedure for aggregated analysis that yielded minimal standard error bias, compared to unacceptably large standard error bias performing SEM analysis on a complex sample with traditional ML fitting methods based on normal theory. Kaplan and Ferguson and Bentler and Chou (1987) reported that probability weights should be used in SEM analysis of data from complex sample designs to reduce parameter estimation bias and support more accurate inferences. As noted by Kaplan and others, standard errors are underestimated even when sampling weights are applied. Thus, while using supplied case weights will help reduce bias, the problem of the *design effect* (deff) remains.

The "design effect" is the ratio of the variance of a statistic under a given sample design to the variance for the same statistic given a simple random sample of equal size. For example, the average increase in sampling variances for estimates (i.e., the design effects) from the 1995 SCS was approximately 2.0, according to a Department of Census statistician familiar with the 1995 SCS (T. Mattingly, personal communication, July 2, 1998). This value varies by variable and by type of statistic, with somewhat lower values for subgroup estimates. Inferential statistical procedures that are carried out without addressing design effect run the risk of producing incorrect results. National scale datasets such as the SCS and NCVS have included Generalized Variance Formula information in the dataset documents, providing researchers with a workaround to address design effect and conduct inferential statistical procedures using such complex survey datasets. At the same time, the only relevant data to assist the SEM researcher working with such datasets is a weighting variable, which only addresses part of the problem linked to the complex sample design. Aside from hoping that the Z-scores associated with specific SEM model parameter estimates are very large (e.g., > 5), thus rendering most design effect concerns moot, the researcher must consider using more involved bootstrapping and jackknife techniques.

Working with survey data naturally brings other potential problems to bear. Respondents often fail to answer all questions, and researchers must struggle with issues surrounding missing and/or incomplete data. The next section explores concerns of missing data and imputation.

MISSING DATA AND IMPUTATION PROCEDURES

In addition to having nonrespondents in surveys, completed surveys almost always result in some missing data, sometimes from overt nonresponse on particular questions, "don't know" types of responses, uncodable responses resulting in "out of universe" codes, and data collection and/or transcription errors. Two fundamental approaches to deal with missing data are (a) some variation of a Maximum Likelihood approach of calculating target statistics from available data, essentially performing estimates for the complete sample; and (b) data imputation, in which predicted data values are actually inserted into empty cells to be later subject to statistical analysis along with the original source data. Procedures exist for analyzing data classified as Missing Completely at Random (MCAR) and Missing at Random (MAR) (Dunn, Everitt, & Pickles, 1993). Likewise, pairwise and listwise deletion methods are available in statistical analysis software, but such procedures, especially pairwise deletion, can cause serious problems (Kaplan, 2000; Marsh, 1998).

This points to a dilemma often encountered in survey research. On the one hand, it may be viewed as risky to engage in data imputation to preserve numerous cases that are complete on many other variables. On the other hand, when large numbers of cases are at risk for deletion, the researcher must consider whether the cases embody some systematic differences that may impair the subsequent analysis. The second approach mentioned above, data imputation, can employ methods as simple as insertion of mean values (highly problematic and inadvisable), but more often, with some more formal predictive algorithm, such as a saturated regression model (using all other measured variables in the model) and automatic addition of a random error (noise) term, thus preserving the case count.

Mayer and Leone (1999) employed an ad hoc cross-validation approach to address the missing data issue. In addition to performing SEM analysis on a complete group ($N = 6,947$) for which missing values were imputed using a saturated regression approach with random noise added, the researchers performed SEM analysis on a so-called "pure" subset of cases ($N = 2,649$) for which complete data existed, requiring no data imputation. Both analyses yielded models with excellent fit and very similar solutions. This procedure provided an additional level of support for the findings. Missing data remains a critical concern of survey researchers in the social sciences, and threats of bias and precision must be considered. A significant body of SEM methodological literature addresses this and related issues.

HYPOTHESIS TESTING AND FIT INDICES

Part of any structural equation analysis involves examination of chi-square statistics to aid in hypotheses testing to help decide whether to reject or fail to reject the specified model. Fit indices such as the Comparative Fit Index (CFI) and RMSEA are used to ascertain goodness of fit. A problem with reporting probability estimates based on the model chi-square values is that the chi-square distribution is sensitive to large sample size. As a result, even trivial misspecification of a model with a large N will lead the researcher to usually reject the proposed model, because invariably, the p-values will be less than .05 (Hu & Bentler, 1995; Loehlin, 1992; Raykov & Widaman, 1995). In this case, the chi-square is really a "badness of fit" test (Hoyle, 1995), and ideally, to not reject the proposed model, the researcher would like to see the p-values associated with the model chi-square statistic be larger than .05. Furthermore, the chi-square test is limited to a dichotomous decision regarding the hypothesis and offers no utility in measuring degree of fit. As a result, many researchers do not focus so much on the p-values associated with model chi-square statistics, but rather, address fit indices and tests of significance of model parameters.

SEM researchers rely heavily on fit indices, which assess the degree of correspondence between the hypothesized model and actual data. Hu and Bentler (1995) discussed three basic problems associated with fit indices in SEM: (a) bias linked to small samples, (b) estimation effects, and (c) violations of assumptions of normality and independence. Fit indices can be roughly grouped into *absolute*, *incremental*, and *parsimonious* categories. The Goodness-of-Fit Index (GFI) and Adjusted Goodness-of-Fit Index (AGFI) are examples of absolute fit indices. They can be sensitive to small sample size and poor model specification and thus are generally avoided. Basic disadvantages of absolute fit indices include (a) not accounting for model complexity in assessing fit, (b) poor performance associated with small sample size, and (c) poor performance associated with violations of normality. Another subset of absolute fit indices that compares predicted versus observable covariances are the Root Mean Square Residuals (RMSR) and the Standardized Root Mean Square Residuals (SRMSR). These two indices provide a direct measure (the latter standardized) of the square root of the difference between predicted and measured variances/covariances in the analysis. Browne, MacCallum, Kim, Andersen, and Glaser (2002) discussed potential incompatibilities and contradictions that can arise when using residual-based indices with other measures of fit.

Incremental measures such as the Normed Fit Index (NFI), Non-Normed Fit index (NNFI), the Comparative Fit Index (CFI), and others have been used to assess model fit based on comparison to a null (independence) model in which all variables are assumed to be completely independent and no covariances can exist among model elements. The NFI and NNFI each have problems that make them generally less desirable measures of fit compared to the CFI. The CFI, which can have values from 0 to 1, reports larger values for better model fit. Conventional wisdom has suggested that a value of .95 be used as a cutoff score for good model performance under the CFI. Hu and Bentler (1999) offered specific suggestions of cutoff values for using particular combinations of fit indices, including the CFI. The most common examples of parsimonious fit indices are Akaike's Information Criterion (AIC) and Bozdogan's Consistent Information Criterion (CAIC), which compute model fit, taking into account degrees of freedom and number of variances/covariances in the model.

Dozens of fit indices are reported by SEM software, and the task of deciding which are most appropriate for analysis and reporting purposes can be somewhat daunting. Most researchers report and discuss multiple measures of fit, often focusing on the CFI, RMSEA, and AIC. The reader is referred to Hu and Bentler (1995, 1999) for an extended discussion of this topic.

STRUCTURED MEANS MODELING AND LAGRANGE TESTS OF VALIDITY OF CONSTRAINTS

Structured Means Modeling (SMM) requires a test of the validity of constraints (see Figure 2). This approach (Hancock, 1997), which does not combine the data from the two groups, uses slopes (paths from latent constructs to measured variables) and intercepts (paths from the V999 constant with a value of 1–in EQS software–to measured variables and constructs) associated with the relationships among the measured variables and constructs to estimate means for the latent constructs. Normally, both slopes and intercepts are constrained to be equal across groups to facilitate a meaningful comparison and also to address the issue of model underidentification. Estimation of latent means with structured means modeling can be problematic (Bentler, 1995; Dunn et al., 1993). Problems with lower fit, variation in latent means estimation, and erratic behavior of Lagrange Multiplier tests of validity of constraints can emerge, possibly necessitating modifications to the normal estimation procedures.

Mayer (2001) faced all three of these problems in an analysis of 1995 and 1999 SCS data and developed an ad hoc approach to facilitate a meaningful analysis. Two series of structured means analyses were performed. First, a series of 130 structured means analysis runs were conducted in which slopes were not constrained across groups but intercepts were constrained, using every possible available combination (beyond those paths from factors to measured variables that were set equal to 1 for scale estimation purposes) of releasing one, two, or three constraints. This was done due to an initial low CFI value of model fit and estimation problems with Lagrange tests. A stable pattern of significant latent mean estimates emerged with a median robust CFI of 0.94. Effect sizes for changes in the latent means were calculated (Hancock, 2001). The reported effect sizes represent differences in standard deviation units between the latent means for 1995 and 1999.

A second series of 24 structured means analysis runs were performed, constraining all paths (above and beyond those fixed to a value of "1" for scale identification purposes). These runs were conducted due to known difficulty reaching stable estimates (Bentler, 1995) and unstable performance of Lagrange tests resulting from choosing alternative fixed value paths. The 24 runs used every possible combination of paths set equal to a value of "1" for scale identification. Sixteen of the 24 runs had no condition code problems while eight of the runs exhibited linear dependency problems.

The combination of these two ad hoc procedures allowed the researcher to have a "sliding window view" into the validity of constraints, establishing a clear overall pattern of stable estimates that simply was not available with an omnibus approach. Interestingly,

Bentler (1995) commented as to the unpopularity of SMM techniques specifically due to stability problems in the analyses.

While these and other technical details of SMM and SEM analysis can pose considerable challenges to the researcher, on a more substantive level, the analyst must consider the deeper meaning tied to the SEM model. The difficulties and challenges of modeling complex social phenomena are discussed in the next section.

DEVELOPING VIABLE INTERPRETATIONS OF COMPLEX SOCIAL PHENOMENA

Researchers often seek to reduce complex human behaviors into elegant structural models that flow from real-world data. While highly seductive, especially in this age of easy-to-use powerful statistical analysis software, the investigator must keep several basic cautions in mind. First, structural equation models do not in and of themselves prove the existence of causal relationships. When based on prior research, sound theory, solid data, and appropriate implementation, SEM analysis can provide firm support for hypotheses regarding social processes, but nothing more.

Second, researchers must remain cognizant about the tendency to capitalize on chance (Bentler & Chou, 1987; MacCallum, 1995; Rakov & Widaman, 1995). That is to say, SEM analysis should generally be based on models specified a priori. Researchers may be tempted to first engage in exploratory analysis followed by confirmatory methods, seeking to uncover and later "justify" relationships in the data. Aside from generally being "bad science," such approaches fall prey to inherent weakness of techniques based on correlational structures–confirmable relationships can emerge that may or may not represent functional and appropriate models of a process under study (Cliff, 1983).

Third, the "nominalistic fallacy" (Cliff, 1983) is the tendency for the investigator to assume that by virtue of naming and categorizing a variable, that it is somehow understood on a functional level. The linkage of real-world measured variables and theoretical constructs contained within the researcher's SEM model can be somewhat tenuous at best. Problems of reliability and validity of measures associated with latent constructs are ever present.

Fourth, most social phenomena are rather complex. Experts who study school violence generally acknowledge that schoolchildren exist within a nested ecology (Tolan & Guerra, 1994) with multiple influences interacting in a dynamic system over time. SEM analysis of processes associated with school violence cannot fully address such complex models, and data-gathering requirements to support such complex analysis would make this research unrealistic from a cost perspective alone. Given this, SEM research can play a critical role in examining key aspects of school violence, working with subsets of more complex models.

CONCLUSION

Structural equation modeling and structured means modeling provide researchers with valuable tools to help explicate relationships and processes associated with violence and disruption in the schools. While not sufficient to "prove" causal relationships, SEM techniques can provide strong evidence that clarifies our understanding of these phenomena. Valuable nationwide data relating to school violence (e.g., School Crime Supplement) is collected on an ongoing basis, providing researchers with opportunities for investigation. Such investigation can be fruitful, provided that methodological strengths and limitations are understood and accommodated. Challenges remain while using SEM methodology, especially with regard to measurement properties of indicator variables, sample design, multiyear surveys, missing data, model testing, and modeling complex social phenomena.

This article has introduced several basic methodological considerations in performing SEM research of school violence and related processes. While the tenor of many parts of the discussion may at first glance seem discouraging, suggesting that the SEM researcher can become beleaguered with multiple problems, that is not really the case. As with other forms of advanced statistical research, the investigator must be well versed in the methodology, addressing limitations in the data and understand trade-offs in the analytic framework. For an extensive list of SEM methodological articles, the reader is referred to <http://www.upa.pdx.edu/IOA/newsom/semrefs.htm>.

REFERENCES

Bentler, P. M. (1995). *EQS structural equations program manual.* Encino, CA: Multivariate Software, Inc.
Bentler, P. M., & Chou, C-P. (1987). Practical issues in structural modeling. *Sociological Methods & Research, 16*(1), 78-117.

Browne, M. W., MacCallum, R. C., Kim, C.-T., Andersen, B. L., & Glaser, R. (2002). When fit indices and residuals are incompatible. *Psychological Methods, 7*(4), 403-421.

Cliff, N. (1983). Some cautions concerning the application of causal modeling methods. *Multivariate Behavioral Research, 18*(1), 115-26.

Dunn, G., Everitt, B., & Pickles, A. (1993). *Modelling covariances and latent variables using EQS.* London: Chapman & Hall.

Gottfredson, G. D., & Gottfredson, D. C. (1985). *Victimization in schools.* New York: Plenum.

Hancock, G. R. (2001). Effect size, power, and sample size determination for structured means modeling and MIMIC approaches to between-groups hypothesis testing of means on a single latent construct. *Psychometrika, 66*(3), 373-388.

Hoyle, R. H. (1995). The structural equation modeling approach: Basic concepts and fundamental issues. In R. H. Hoyle (Ed.), *Structural equation modeling: Concepts, issues, and applications* (pp. 1-15). Thousand Oaks, CA: Sage.

Hoyle, R. H., & Smith, G. T. (1994). Formulating clinical research hypotheses as structural equation models: A conceptual overview. *Journal of Consulting and Clinical Psychology, 62*(3), 429-440.

Hu, L., & Bentler, P. M. (1995). Evaluating model fit. In R. H. Hoyle (Ed.), *Structural equation modeling: Concepts, issues, and applications* (pp. 76-99). Thousand Oaks, CA: Sage.

Hu, L., & Bentler, P. M. (1999). Cutoff criteria for fit indexes in covariance structure analysis: Conventional criteria versus new alternatives. *Structural Equation Modeling, 6*(1), 1-55.

Kaplan, D. (2000). *Structural equation modeling: Foundations and extensions.* Thousand Oaks, CA: Sage.

Kaplan, D., & Ferguson, A. J. (1999). On the utilization of sample weights in latent variable models. *Structural Equation Modeling, 6*(4), 305-321.

Karcher, M. J. (2002). The cycle of violence and disconnection among rural middle school students: Teacher disconnection as a consequence of violence. *Journal of School Violence, 1*(1), 35-51.

Kish, L. (1965). *Survey sampling.* New York: Wiley.

Kish, L., & Frankel, M. (1974). Inference from complex samples. *Journal of the Royal Statistical Society, Series B, 36,* 1-37.

Loehlin, J. C. (1992). *Latent variable models: An introduction to factor, path, and structural analysis* (2nd ed.). Hillsdale, NJ: Lawrence Erlbaum.

MacCallum, R. C. (1995). Model specification: Procedures, strategies, and related issues. In R. H. Hoyle (Ed.), *Structural equation modeling: Concepts, issues, and applications* (pp. 16-36). Thousand Oaks, CA: Sage.

Mandell, D. J., Hill, S. L., Carter, L., & Brandon, R. N. (2002). *The impact of substance use and violence/delinquency on academic achievement for groups of middle and high school students in Washington.* Seattle, WA: UW Human Services Policy Center, Washington Kids Count.

Marsh, H. W. (1998). Pairwise deletion for missing data in structural equation models: Nonpositive definite matrices, parameter estimates, goodness of fit, and adjusted sample sizes. *Structural Equation Modeling, 5*(1), 22-36.

Mayer, M. J. (2001). *The relationship of secure building strategies and students' understanding of the school's system of law to school violence and disruption.* Dissertation Abstracts International, *62/12,* 4057.

Mayer, M. J., & Leone, P. E. (1999). A structural analysis of school violence and disruption: Implications for creating safer schools. *Education and Treatment of Children, 22,* 333-358.

Muthen, B. O., & Satorra, A. (1995). Complex sample data in structural equation modeling. In P. V. Marsden (Ed.), *Sociological methodology 1995* (pp. 267-316). Washington, DC: American Sociological Association.

Raykov, T., & Widaman, K. F. (1995). Issues in applied structural equation modeling research. *Structural Equation Modeling, 2*(4), 289-318.

Tolan, P. H., & Guerra, N. G. (1994). Prevention of delinquency: Current status and issues. *Applied & Preventive Psychology, 3,* 251-273.

West, S. G., Finch, J. F., & Curran, P. J. (1995). Structural equation models with nonnormal variables: Problems and remedies. In R. H. Hoyle (Ed.), *Structural equation modeling: Concepts, issues, and applications* (pp. 56-75). Thousand Oaks, CA: Sage.

Beyond Guns, Drugs and Gangs: The Structure of Student Perceptions of School Safety

Russell Skiba
Ada B. Simmons
Reece Peterson
Janet McKelvey
Susan Forde
Sarah Gallini

Russell Skiba is affiliated with the Department of Counseling and Educational Psychology, Indiana University.

Ada B. Simmons is affiliated with the Center for Evaluation and Education Policy, Indiana University.

Reece Peterson is affiliated with the Department of Special Education, University of Nebraska-Lincoln.

Janet McKelvey, Susan Forde, and Sarah Gallini are affiliated with the Center for Evaluation and Education Policy, Indiana University.

Address correspondence to: Russell Skiba, Indiana University, Center for Evaluation and Education Policy, 509 E. Third Street, Bloomington, IN 47401 (E-mail: skiba@indiana.edu).

The authors wish to acknowledge the assistance of Kimberly Boone and Angela Fontanini, graduate research assistants at the Indiana Education Policy Center, and Courtney Miller at the University of Nebraska for their assistance in data collection, and Cyndi Skoog, Forest Hills Special Education Cooperative, for her assistance in school district coordination.

This article and the products it describes were developed with support from grant H325N990009 from the Office of Special Education Programs, United States Department of Education.

[Haworth co-indexing entry note]: "Beyond Guns, Drugs and Gangs: The Structure of Student Perceptions of School Safety." Skiba, Russell et al. Co-published simultaneously in *Journal of School Violence* (The Haworth Press, Inc.) Vol. 3, No. 2/3, 2004. pp. 149-171; and: *Issues in School Violence Research* (ed: Michael J. Furlong et al.) The Haworth Press, Inc., 2004, pp. 149-171. Single or multiple copies of this article are available for a fee from The Haworth Document Delivery Service [1-800-HAWORTH, 9:00 a.m. - 5:00 p.m. (EST). E-mail address: docdelivery@haworthpress.com].

http://www.haworthpress.com/web/JSV
© 2004 by The Haworth Press, Inc. All rights reserved.
Digital Object Identifier: 10.1300/J202v03n02_09

SUMMARY. The failure to consider factors that make a key contribution to violence and its prevention may create serious problems of construct validity for school violence surveys. Further, few studies have assessed the relative importance of variables contributing to perceptions of safety by examining correlations between survey items and overall feelings of school safety. This study describes the development of a self-report survey, the *Safe and Responsive Schools Safe School Survey*, explicitly designed to assess perceptions regarding criminal violation and serious violence as well as day-to-day disruption and climate issues. Principal components analysis identified four factors involving student connectedness, incivility, feelings of personal safety, and delinquency/major safety. Further multivariate analysis suggests that, in at least some cases, feelings about connectedness and climate may be more critical than serious violence in shaping student perceptions of school safety. *[Article copies available for a fee from The Haworth Document Delivery Service: 1-800-HAWORTH. E-mail address: <docdelivery@ haworthpress.com> Website: <http://www.HaworthPress.com> © 2004 by The Haworth Press, Inc. All rights reserved.]*

KEYWORDS. Survey, school violence, methodological, school safety, school climate, violence prevention

INTRODUCTION

Self-report measures assessing student perceptions of violence and their own personal sense of safety at school have been among the most widely used measures for assessing school violence (Furlong & Morrison, 1994, 2000). Some have argued the direct approach afforded by such surveys represents the most practical and ethical measure of obtaining school violence data (Fitzgerald & Mulford, 1986). Student self-report surveys may be more precise than community-based data (e.g., police reports or emergency room records), while at the same time affording a higher degree of anonymity to respondents (Kingery, Coggeshall, & Alford, 1998).

Yet a number of limitations of self-report surveys have been identified, including errors in reporting, motivation to report accurately, overreporting and underreporting (Bruce & Desmond, 1997; Eisenhower, Mathiowetz, & Morganstein, 1991; Newfield, 1980). Specific concerns have also been raised about the reliability of particular subsets of respondents on school safety surveys. Studies that have specifically explored student response patterns have reported rates of incomplete or unreliable student reporting that may be quite high (Cornell & Loper, 1998). Nor are such patterns distributed randomly: Students who failed reliability checks were also more likely to report higher rates of victimization and perceptions of danger (Rosenblatt & Furlong, 1997).

While such concerns address the accuracy and reliability of self-report, there may also be reasons to be concerned about the construct validity of self-report measures of school violence or safety. Unless school safety surveys represent a relatively complete universe of variables that have been identified as contributing to school safety (see e.g., Leone, Mayer, Malmgren, & Meisel 2000; Walker et al., 1996), the scale will be unable to assess factors that make important contributions to student perceptions of violence or safety. In addition, although it is typically assumed that certain events or behaviors, such as weapons possession, are highly influential in determining whether a school is perceived to be safe, few surveys have assessed the actual correlations between specific items and overall feelings of school safety.

The purpose of this study was to explore the structure of student perceptions of school safety through a theoretically comprehensive school safety survey, the *Safe and Responsive Schools (SRS) Safe Schools Survey*. In order to assess the overlap between the measurement of school safety and school climate, we begin by reviewing some existing school safety and school climate surveys.

Measures of School Safety

A number of surveys assessing student perception of the extent of violence or the overall safety of their school have been reported in the literature (Chandler, Chapman, Rand, & Taylor, 1998; Cornell & Loper, 1998; Furlong, Chung, Bates, & Morrison, 1995; Kann et al., 2000; Resnick et al., 1997; Shoffner & Vacc, 1999). Although definitions of school violence have broadened considerably in the last decade beyond juvenile justice violation or physical assault (Flannery, 1997; Furlong & Morrison, 2000), the majority of available school safety surveys maintain a narrow focus on actual or potential criminal violations and occurrences of physical harm. Thus, the most common items and factors across these scales address the frequency and/or severity of school-related serious violence or criminal violation, including possession and use of weapons, physical assault, substance abuse, rape, and murder. With some exceptions (Cornell & Loper, 1998; Furlong et al., 1995), most extant school violence surveys do not include items assessing the contribution of school climate to student perceptions of school safety.

Moreover, the general absence of an empirical basis for the organization of school safety survey items is of some concern. In survey development, best practice demands that the dimensions or subscales of the measure be identified empirically, through factor analysis or similar multivariate procedures (Cortina, 1993; Gardner, 1995). Yet of the school violence surveys currently reported in the literature, only one (Shoffner & Vacc, 1999) has reported using a statistical procedure such as factor analysis to empirically classify the variables represented by survey items. In the absence of information to the contrary, one must assume that subscales on the remaining surveys were chosen solely on the basis of researcher judgment.

School Climate Measures

Among numerous self-report scales developed to measure the construct of school climate (Lehr & Christenson, 2002), a number of common themes run through the most widely used scales (Fox et al., 1973; Gottfredson, 1991; Haynes, Emmons, Ben-Avie, & Comer, 1996; Karatzias, Power, & Swanson, 2001; NASSP, 1986). Typical factors in these school climate surveys include teacher-student relationships, student-peer relationships, order and discipline, environmental and school building characteristics, parent involvement, support, fairness of rules, and overall student perceptions.

Although most of these surveys are intended to represent a broad range of variables that contribute to perceptions of the adequacy of school climate, few include items or dimensions designed specifically to address the presence or absence of violence as part of a school's climate. The *School Climate Survey* (Haynes et al., 1996) includes a dimension measuring Order and Discipline, while *The Effective School Battery* (Gottfredson, 1991) addresses issues of school safety and major acts of violence through items addressing theft, attacks, robbery, and threats. In general, however, most existing school climate surveys do not include items or dimensions assessing of the impact of school violence or school discipline on perceptions of school climate.

Empirical derivation of subscales appears to be more common among measures of school climate than among measures of school safety. Of the five commonly used scales identified above, three (Haynes et al., 1996; Karatzias et al., 2001; NASSP, 1986) reported the results of a factor analysis for identifying the structure of the subscales.

THEORETICAL MODELS AND SAFETY SURVEYS: CAN WE FIND WHAT WE DON'T MEASURE?

With a few notable exceptions, the measurements of school safety and school climate have been surprisingly independent of one another. School safety surveys tend not to include items assessing the contribution of day-to-day climate variables to school safety perceptions. Conversely, many school climate surveys do not include items measuring the potential contribution of school violence to perceptions of school climate. In contrast, most current theoretical models of the prediction and prevention of youth violence inherently recognize the importance of day-to-day interactions that define school climate in shaping both the perception and reality of school violence or school safety. In the field of delinquency, the social development model formulated by Hawkins and his colleagues (Hawkins, Farrington, & Catalano, 1998) focuses on the central role of school alienation/school connection in the developmental course of juvenile delinquency. In the field of school violence, some variant of a three-tiered prevention model (primary, secondary, and tertiary) presented in Figure 1 appears to be the most typical framework for organizing and understanding school violence and violence prevention efforts (Dwyer, Osher, & Warger, 1998; Larson, 1994; Leone et al., 2000; Walker et al., 1996). With its emphasis on prevention and early intervention, the three-tiered primary prevention model highlights the interconnectedness of school climate and school violence, and the role of day-to-day disruption and feelings of school connection in predicting and preventing more serious incidents of disruption and violence.

It might be argued that criminal violations and physical violence represent the criterion variables in school violence and, hence, the most important variables for measurement on school safety surveys. Yet consistently documented relationships between day-to-day disruption and more serious violence suggest there is some methodological risk involved in surveying only serious violence. National data show a strong positive relationship between the presence of discipline problems and the presence of crime (Heaviside, Rowand, Williams, & Farris, 1998). Comprehensive analyses of targeted violence in schools (Vossekuil et al., 2002) have concluded that deadly violence occurs within the context of the overall school climate, and may often be the end link of a causal chain set in motion by an excess of student harassment and incivility. Indeed, criminal violations and deadly violence represent very low frequency events in most schools and may not be present at all in many schools (DeVoe et al., 2002; Heaviside et al., 1998). As a low frequency event, serious or deadly violence may thus lack

FIGURE 1. The Safe and Responsive Schools Model of school violence prevention (Skiba & Peterson, 2003). Primary prevention approaches to create a
safe and positive school climate are applied universally, addressing issues of
day-to-day disruption and school climate. Secondary prevention strategies of
early identification and early intervention are applied to a smaller proportion of
the school population that may be at risk for violence or disruption, while effective response strategies and intervention are in place for those students who
are already engaging in disruptive behavior.

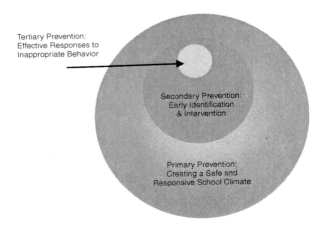

sufficient variability to be a suitable measure of school safety across a
range of schools.

Thus, the general absence of indicators of day-to-day disciplinary disruption or school climate may pose a serious threat to the validity of school
safety surveys. Unless both serious violence and daily disruption/climate
variables are represented on the same survey, there is simply no way to assess the relative importance of those dimensions to overall perceptions of
school safety. It is not uncommon in descriptions of school violence to use
a single item (e.g., "I have seen a knife or a gun at school") as an indicator
of overall perceptions of school safety, assuming that certain events or variables are natural indicators of students' feelings of safety. Yet we are unaware of any previous investigation that has empirically investigated the
relationship between particular events or variables and the criterion, overall
feelings of safety. Thus, the validity of school safety surveys has been for
the most part assumed rather than tested; in truth, we do not know which
events or variables cause students to feel more or less safe in schools.

This article reports on the development and technical characteristics of a comprehensive measure of school safety, the *Safe and Responsive Schools (SRS) Safe Schools Survey*, constructed specifically to assess both serious violence and daily disruption/school climate. In order to test the theoretical rationale for a broader prevention model, we present the factor structure of this composite instrument. Finally, as a test of the validity of a school safety measure scale, we explore the relative importance of measures of serious violence/disruption, school climate, and incivility through a hierarchical linear regression predicting students' overall perceptions of school safety from items drawn from the various factors.

METHOD

Development of the Survey

The *SRS Safe Schools Survey* was constructed to assess the perceptions of students, school staff, and parents concerning school safety and school climate. Three versions of the survey were developed for separate use with parents, school staff, and students (elementary and secondary versions); only the results of the secondary student version are reported here.

The survey was intended to be representative of a comprehensive model of school safety, providing data concerning perceptions of both serious/violent offenses as well as more routine interactions among individuals in the school community. The survey drew upon previous national surveys of school violence that emphasize serious violence or criminal acts (1995 School Crime Supplement Questionnaire; Principal/Disciplinarian Survey on School Violence), and also from existing school climate surveys (School Climate Survey [Form A]; Survey of Learning Climate in Elementary Schools; The Bully Survey) in order to assess the impact of climate and day-to-day events on perceptions of school safety (Crawford & Bodine, 1996; Kelly et al., 1986; Lincoln Public Schools, 1998; McDermott, 1998; NCES, 1996; Swearer & Paulk, 1998; U.S. DOE, 1995, 1998).

From these scales, a pool of 120 items was reduced to 65 items after accounting for redundancy. A pilot test was conducted in five schools in the 1999-2000 school year. Item analysis further reduced the number of items from 65 to 45 items. The final secondary student version included 43 items related to school climate and safety. Two additional items were included as a check on the veracity and seriousness of responding, as recommended in previous literature (Cornell & Loper, 1998; Rosenblatt & Furlong, 1997): *I am reading and responding to this survey carefully* and *My answers to these questions accurately reflect my feelings.* Questions were framed as a 5-point Likert-type scale ranging from strongly disagree (1) to strongly agree (5). Seven additional demographic items included school name, student's race, age, grade level, length of time at the school, and mode of transportation to school.

Participants

The secondary survey was administered during the spring 2001 semester to students in two junior high/middle schools and three high schools in two midwestern states. All of the schools were located in rural/suburban locales or small towns. In two high schools and in two junior high/middle schools, students completed a paper-and-pencil version of the survey; in the third high school, students completed an online version of the survey in the school computer lab. The survey was administered during the school day. An option to decline to participate was available to all students; fewer than 10 students at each school did so.

Copies of the survey and a letter inviting participation were distributed during the school day to students in four of the schools. In order to increase the veracity of student responding, project staff administered the anonymous surveys (Kingery et al., 1998) in one class period of the day, typically English. Students placed their completed surveys in envelopes, which were collected by project staff. In the fifth school, both the invitation to participate and the survey were accessible through the Internet. Students in that school completed the survey in the school computer lab with their class, and completed surveys were transmitted electronically to a secure account established as a data repository.

Response rates for each of the schools surveyed ranged from 59.3% to 86.8% of total enrollment. Nine cases where students completed less than two-thirds of the survey items were dropped, as were 138 cases where respondents strongly disagreed with either of the two veracity items. These deletions yielded a final data set of 2,465 (94.4% of respondents) middle/junior high and high school students. On the factor analysis and regression completed for this study, cases with missing data on any of the survey items were dropped. The factor analysis included 2,231 cases, and the regression included 2,277 cases for net losses less than 15% of the data set due to missing data.

RESULTS

Descriptives

Demographics for the sample are presented in Table 1. The sample represented grades 6-12, with the largest representation from students in grades 9 (21.2%) and 10 (20.1%). Two-thirds of the sample was high school students and the remaining third was middle and junior high school students. The sample was nearly equal in gender representation.

TABLE 1. Sample Demographic Characteristics

		%
School Level	Middle/Junior High	34.3
	High School	65.7
Grade Level	6th	7.8
	7th	13.7
	8th	12.7
	9th	21.2
	10th	20.1
	11th	14.2
	12th	10.2
Gender	Male	48.6
	Female	51.4
Race	White	92.5
	African American	.8
	Hispanic	1.1
	Native American	.7
	Asian/Pacific Islander	1.0
	Biracial/Multiracial	1.7
	Other	2.1
Years in School	1	29.7
	2	30.3
	3	18.4
	4 or More	21.6
Transportation to School	Car	56.8
	Bus	39.5
	Walk	2.0
	Other	1.7

Over 90% of the sample was white; 4.1% of the sample were biracial, multiracial, or other; and the remaining 5.4% were African American, Hispanic, Native Americans, and Asian/Pacific Islander.

The difference in the number of cases included in the descriptive analysis and later factor analysis and regression merits further explanation. The deletion of cases with missing data from factor and regression analyses is typically not regarded as a serious issue so long as the deleted cases are random and few. However, prior research on school violence suggests that students with less accurate or valid patterns of responding may be more likely to have more negative perspectives on the climate and safety of their school (Cornell & Loper, 1998; Rosenblatt & Furlong, 1997), a pattern which violates the criterion of randomness. In this study, we tested for differences in survey completion by dividing the sample into two groups, those with incomplete responses (e.g., any items on the survey left blank) and those with complete responses. Analyses included *t*-tests to assess whether mean differences on any survey items were statistically significant across the two groups. In general, students who completed less than the complete survey tended to have more negative views about the safety of their schools. Statistically significant differences ($p \leq .05$) between complete and incomplete responders were evident on 12 of the 43 survey items dealing with school safety. Students with incomplete survey data were significantly less likely to feel safe according to five of the personal safety items and the item assessing overall feelings of safety, more likely to report having seen a gun at school, and less likely to feel they belonged at their school. They were also less likely to agree that hassling, name calling, and cheating were regular occurrences at school. Thus in order to avoid biasing descriptive results by excluding students with less positive views, we included incomplete responders in our report of descriptive characteristics, although they were dropped from the subsequent factor and regression analyses.

Means for each question on the survey are presented in Table 2. In general, students felt their schools were safe, with a mean of 3.55 on the item and 58.0% of students agreeing or strongly agreeing with the statement *Overall, I feel that this school is a safe school.* They felt safest coming and going from school (3.88), in the lunchroom (3.87), in their classrooms (3.78), and on school grounds (3.76). Students assigned their highest rates of agreement with statements that acknowledged routine mild verbal harassment among students: name calling, insults, and teasing (4.26), drug and alcohol use by students outside of school

TABLE 2. Means of Safe Schools Survey Items

Descriptive Statistics	Mean	Std. Deviation	N
I am reading and responding to this survey carefully	4.59	0.67	2465
My answers to these questions accurately reflect my feelings	4.50	0.74	2465
Name calling, insults, or teasing happen regularly at school	4.26	0.91	2455
Students use drugs or alcohol outside of school	4.20	1.10	2458
Arguments among students are common at school	4.08	0.97	2444
Some students are regularly hassled by other students	3.88	1.01	2452
I feel safe going to and coming from school	3.88	1.02	2444
I feel safe in the lunchroom	3.87	1.03	2454
I feel safe in my classrooms	3.78	1.00	2454
I feel safe before and after school while on school grounds	3.76	1.03	2457
I feel safe in the school hallways	3.65	1.05	2454
Students cut classes or are absent regularly	3.62	1.14	2451
Students regularly cheat on tests or assignments	3.62	1.13	2452
Teachers and administrators supervise the halls during passing time	3.60	1.09	2458
I feel safe in the bathrooms at school	3.58	1.13	2459
Overall, I feel that this school is a safe school	3.55	1.07	2449
Groups of students cause problems or conflicts at school	3.54	1.11	2458
I have seen students smoking at school or on school grounds	3.53	1.49	2454
Threats by one student against another are common at school	3.53	1.08	2461
I feel that teachers care about my learning	3.48	1.07	2446
School rules are clearly defined and explained so that I can understand them	3.44	1.16	2446
Teachers and staff accept me for who I am	3.43	1.15	2457
I am getting a good education at this school	3.36	1.06	2459
I am generally treated fairly at this school	3.35	1.14	2449
I feel that I belong at this school	3.30	1.18	2448
Teachers praise students when they have done well	3.28	1.00	2458
I feel welcome when I am at school	3.27	1.12	2459
I am learning a lot at this school	3.26	1.11	2456
I feel that I can talk to a teacher or an administrator if I have a problem	3.25	1.19	2462
Robbery or theft of school property over $10 in value is common	3.21	1.18	2459
Physical fighting or conflicts happen regularly at school	3.16	1.08	2453
I feel that the teachers care about me as a person	3.15	1.12	2457
I am proud of this school	3.15	1.19	2451
Teachers enjoy teaching here	3.13	1.05	2455
I have seen students with drugs or alcohol at school	3.10	1.45	2454
Sale of drugs occurs on school grounds	3.05	1.35	2453
Teachers listen carefully to what I have to say	3.04	1.05	2455
Students use alcohol or drugs at school	2.99	1.28	2451
I feel comfortable telling a teacher or an administrator about potential violence	2.95	1.19	2458
School rules seem reasonable	2.94	1.21	2454
Teachers work hard to make every student successful	2.93	1.14	2454
I have seen a knife at school (not including a cafeteria knife)	2.82	1.43	2448
Students enjoy learning here	2.70	1.09	2460
Most students are proud of this school	2.60	1.08	2454
I have seen a gun at school this year	1.50	0.94	2454
Age	15.06	1.76	2445
Years in this school	2.32	1.12	2418

(4.20), and frequent arguments among students (4.08). Students also tended to agree that cutting class and cheating were regular parts of school life (3.62 on each item). They were neutral on the presence and use of drugs or alcohol at school (2.99-3.10), and less likely to agree that they had seen weapons at school (knife = 2.82, gun = 1.50).

Compared to their feelings of safety at school, students tended to be more neutral on items that assessed their sense of connection at school and their perceptions of teachers' concern for them on an individual basis. Slightly less than half (48.2%) of the students agreed or strongly agreed with the statement, *I feel I belong at this school.* Although slightly more than half of the students, 52.4%, agreed or strongly agreed that teachers accepted them for who they are, over one-fourth disagreed or strongly disagreed that teachers cared about them as individuals. Students were neutral as to whether teachers were willing to listen carefully to them (3.04) and that teachers were working hard to make every student successful (2.93).

Factor Analysis: The Structure of School Safety Perceptions

To identify the underlying processes that characterized students' perceptions of physical safety and security at school, we performed a principal component factor analysis, a statistical technique that is particularly appropriate for the task of developing an empirical summary of the data set (Tabachnick & Fidell, 1996). Because the correlation between two of the four factors exceeded .32, we chose oblique, rather than orthogonal, rotation as an aid in interpreting the factors that were extracted (Tabachnick & Fidell, 1996). In accordance with convention for oblique rotations, we interpret and report the pattern matrix rather than the structure matrix. This method is similar to standard multiple regression in that it omits shared variance, but facilitates the identification of a set of variables that constitute each factor. In determining the number of factors to be retained, we used a general guide of retaining factors with eigenvalues greater than 1 in conjunction with examination of a scree plot that enabled us to judge the point at which discontinuity in eigenvalues occurred (Tabachnick & Fidell, 1996).

Based on these criteria, four factors emerged from the factor analysis: Connection/Climate, Incivility and Disruption, Personal Safety, and Delinquency/Major Safety. Loadings of the variables on components are presented in Table 3, with variables ordered by size of loading. With a cut point set at .30 for inclusion of a variable in interpretation of a factor in an exploratory study, only one survey item did not load on any factor. Four variables loaded on two components. The variables with

TABLE 3. Factor Loadings from the Principal Components Analysis of the Safe and Responsive Schools Secondary Student Survey

Factor and Variable	Loading
Connection/Climate (Alpha = .939)	
Teachers work hard to make every student successful.	.818
I feel that the teachers care about me as a person.	.817
Teachers listen carefully to what I have to say.	.784
I feel that teachers care about my learning.	.761
Teachers and staff accept me for who I am.	.723
I am learning a lot at this school.	.717
Teachers enjoy teaching here.	.717
I am getting a good education at this school.	.714
Students enjoy learning here.	.701
I feel comfortable telling a teacher or an administrator about potential violence.	.669
Teachers praise students when they have done well.	.660
I feel that I can talk to a teacher or administrator if I have a problem.	.654
School rules seem reasonable.	.648
I am proud of this school.	.619
Most students are proud of this school.	.572
I feel welcome when I am at school.	.560
I feel that I belong at this school.	.535
School rules are clearly defined and explained so I can understand them.	.518
I am generally treated fairly at my school.	.517
Incivility and Disruption (Alpha = .827)	
Name calling, insults, or teasing happen regularly at school.	.767
Arguments among students are common at school.	.757
Some students are regularly hassled by other students.	.725
Groups of students cause problems or conflicts at school.	.693
Threats by one student against another are common at school.	.603
Physical fighting or conflicts happen regularly at school.	.582
Students regularly cheat on tests or assignments.	.417
Personal Safety (Alpha = .893)	
I feel safe in the school hallways.	.847
I feel safe in the lunchroom.	.777
I feel safe going to and coming from school.	.771
I feel safe in the bathrooms at school.	.769
I feel safe before and after school while on school grounds.	.752
I feel safe in my classrooms.	.710
Overall, I feel that this school is a safe school.	.682
I have seen a gun at school this year.	$-.361$

TABLE 3 (continued)

Factor and Variable	Loading
Delinquency/Major Safety (Alpha = .853)	
Sale of drugs occurs on school grounds.	.816
I have seen students with drugs or alcohol at school.	.805
Students use drugs or alcohol at school.	.801
I have seen students smoking at school or on school grounds.	.733
Students use drugs or alcohol outside of school.	.578
I have seen a knife at school (not including a cafeteria knife).	.537
Students cut classes or are absent regularly.	.471
Robbery or theft of school property over $10 in value is common.	.312

Note. The following item did not load on any of the factors: *Teachers and administrators supervise the halls during passing times.* The following items were not included in the factor analysis: *I am reading and responding to this survey carefully; My answers to these questions accurately reflect my feelings.* The following items loaded on to more than one factor (weaker loadings listed in parentheses): *I feel welcome when I am at school* (.324 on Factor 3); *Students regularly cheat on tests or assignments* (.399 on Factor 4); *Students cut classes or are absent regularly* (.330 on Factor 2); and *Robbery or theft of school property over $10 in value is common* (.305 on Factor 2).

these weaker factor loadings, which ranged from .396 to .306, were included with the components on which they loaded more strongly. Collectively, the four-factor solution accounted for 51.67% of the variance in the variables.

As an estimation of the internal consistency of each factor, Cronbach's alphas were computed for each factor. The lowest reliability, .83, was for the Incivility and Disruption factor. The reliabilities for the other factors were .85 (Delinquency/Major Safety), .89 (Personal Safety), and .94 (Connection/Climate).

The first factor, labeled Connection/Climate, accounted for 28.63% of the variance in the variables–the largest contribution of the four components. This factor contained 19 items that described students' perceptions of the personal concern, fairness, and trust extended to them by school personnel.

Survey items related to Incivility and Disruption made up the second factor, which contributed an additional 11.76% to the explained variance in the variables. These seven variables focused on the civility of interpersonal relationships among students as expressed by the frequency of name calling, arguments, and conflicts.

Eight variables related to Personal Safety loaded on a third factor. The majority of items on this factor directly pertained to assessments of feelings of personal safety in a variety of settings. The one exception was the contribution of seeing a gun at school, which suggests that particular experience impacts feelings of personal safety.

The fourth component, labeled Delinquency/Major Safety, contained six variables that tapped students' awareness of the presence of drugs, alcohol, knives, and smoking on school property. This factor accounted for 4.06% of the total variance.

Predicting Overall Perceptions of School Safety

Inclusion of items in the School Safety Survey that represent the domains of both serious disruption/violence and climate/civility issues provides an opportunity to assess which of these items most strongly predicts overall perceptions of school safety. Thus, we entered the items from the survey into a hierarchical linear regression predicting students' overall perception of safety at their school (*Overall, I feel this school is a safe school*). Items from three of the four components identified by the principal components analysis were entered sequentially as blocks into the model. We excluded the *I feel safe . . .* variables in the Personal Safety component because of their obvious overlap with perceptions of general safety, as evidenced by the strength of their bivariate correlations with the dependent variable.[1] The item, *I have seen a gun at school this year*, was retained for purposes of the regression analysis due to its theoretical importance in perceptions of school safety.

Results of the regression analysis (Table 4) showed that together these variables make a strong contribution to overall perceptions of school safety. Collectively, the three blocks of variables predicted a total of 46.4% of the variance in the outcome variable, and at each step both the block of added variables as well as the entire model was statistically significant. Each column in Table 4 represents the inclusion of a block of variables associated with each of the three survey factors.

Entering the block of variables related to Major Safety in the first step accounted for 12.2% of the predicted variance. Four of the eight variables in model 1 were statistically significant. The significant variables pertained to drugs, alcohol, weapons, and theft at school, with the item, *I have seen a gun at school this year*, making the largest contribution of the variables in the block.

In the second step, we entered the block of variables comprising the factor Incivility/Disruption; together, these items accounted for an additional 7.1% of the variance in perceptions of overall safety. Three of the four variables that were statistically significant in model 1 remained significant, and one additional variable from block 1 became statistically significant in this step. Of the Incivility/Disruption variables entered in this step, arguments, threats, and physical conflicts were statistically sig-

TABLE 4. Summary of Hierarchical Linear Regression for Variables Predicting Overall Safety (n = 2,277)

Variables	Step 1 Major Safety			Step 2 Incivility/Disruption			Step 3 Connection/Climate		
	Unstand. Beta	Stand. Beta	Sig	Unstand. Beta	Stand. Beta	Sig	Unstand. Beta	Stand. Beta	Sig
Students use alcohol or drugs at school	0.026	0.030	-	−0.005	−0.005	-	−0.029	−0.034	-
I have seen drugs or alcohol at school	0.026	0.078	**	0.046	0.061	*	0.029	0.038	-
Sale of drugs occurs on school grounds	−0.003	−0.004	-	−0.016	−0.019	-	−0.019	−0.023	-
I have seen students smoking at school	−0.018	−0.024	-	−0.025	−0.034	-	−0.010	−0.014	-
I have seen a knife at school	0.110	0.144	***	0.087	0.115	***	0.041	0.054	**
Students use drugs/alcohol outside school	−0.029	−0.030	-	−0.051	−0.052	*	−0.028	−0.029	-
I have seen a gun at school this year	0.239	0.205	***	0.196	0.168	***	0.126	0.107	***
Robbery/theft over $10 is common	0.089	0.096	***	0.035	0.037	-	0.024	0.026	-
Arguments common among students				−0.124	−0.112	***	−0.061	−0.055	**
Name calling, insults, or teasing				0.003	0.003	-	−0.040	−0.034	-
Some students regularly hassled				0.010	0.009	-	0.026	0.024	-
Groups cause problems or conflicts				0.002	0.002	-	0.033	0.034	-
Threats are common at school				0.153	0.153	***	0.067	0.067	***
Physical fighting or conflicts regular				0.231	0.228	***	0.158	0.157	***
Students cut classes regularly				0.021	0.023	-	0.010	0.011	-
Students regularly cheat				0.003	0.003	-	−0.013	−0.013	-
Teachers care about me as a person						-	0.057	0.059	*
Teachers work hard for student success						*	−0.055	−0.058	*
Teachers listen carefully to what I say						-	0.011	0.011	-
I am learning a lot at this school						-	−0.019	−0.019	-
I am getting a good education here						***	0.107	0.106	***
Students enjoy learning here						*	0.073	0.073	**
Teachers care about my learning						***	−0.063	−0.063	**
Teachers enjoy teaching here						-	0.018	0.018	-
I am proud of this school						***	0.101	0.110	***
Teachers accept me for who I am						-	−0.014	−0.015	-
Teachers praise students for success						-	0.004	0.003	-
School rules seem reasonable						-	0.031	0.034	-
I can talk to teachers about problems							0.019	0.021	-
I feel comfortable about reporting violence							−0.012	−0.013	-
I feel welcome when I am at school							0.227	0.233	***
Most students are proud of this school							0.030	0.030	-
School rules are clearly defined							0.003	0.003	-
I feel I belong at this school							0.015	0.016	-
I am treated fairly at this school							0.138	0.145	***
Model Statistics	Adj R^2	0.122		Adj R^2	.194		Adj R^2	0.460	
	N	2277		N	2277		N	2277	

* $p < .05$ ** $p < .01$ *** $p < .001$

nificant. Threats and physical conflicts were positively related to feelings of safety; arguments were negatively related to perceptions of safety.

Entering the variables related to the Connection/Climate factor in step 3 resulted in the largest change in R^2 (26.6%) in the model. A number of variables from previous steps remained significant, but two variables, *I have seen drugs or alcohol at school* and *Robbery/theft over $10 is common,* dropped out of the equation by the third step. Eight new variables related to Connection/Climate were statistically significant in model 3, sharing a theme of school connected through teacher caring, student pride and feeling welcome in school. Two items related to teachers' academic orientation (*Teachers work hard for student success* and *Teachers care about my learning*) made significant negative predictions to students' overall feelings of school safety.

In sum, a combination of items related to incivility, school connectedness, and major safety issues were able to account for a substantial proportion of the variance in overall perceptions of school safety. The largest contribution to the overall equation was not items indicative of criminal behavior or serious violence, but rather items assessing perceptions of climate and especially school connection. The largest single contribution to the overall prediction of school safety perceptions was the item, *I feel welcome when I am at school.*

DISCUSSION

These results provide support for a more comprehensive approach to the design of self-report measures of school violence and school safety. Despite a theoretical shift toward more comprehensive models and definitions in the field of school violence (Furlong & Morrison, 2000), the majority of published surveys of school violence, and in particular the most widely reported of those surveys (*School Crime Supplement*–Chandler et al., 1998; *Youth Risk Behavior Surveillance*–Kann et al., 2000) maintain a more narrow focus on delinquency and physical acts of violence. The current results suggest that such an approach may have limited validity in at least some locales in describing the true structure of student perceptions of school safety and school violence. In short, school safety is determined by more than weapons, drugs, and gangs.

These analyses replicate and extend previous findings regarding nonvalid responses on school safety surveys. Previous research has shown that students whose responses are less trustworthy also report higher levels of victimization and violence (Cornell & Loper, 1998;

Rosenblatt & Furlong, 1997). The current results extend those findings, showing that even students with incomplete patterns of responding are more likely to have more negative views about the climate and safety of their school. Such findings pose a difficult problem for self-report methods of school violence assessment; it is impossible to know whether the more extreme responding of incomplete or nonvalid responders is a product of a less serious response set, or whether higher rates of exposure to violence or victimization has led some students to adopt a less serious response set as a kind of defense mechanism.

The main purpose of this report, however, was to explore issues of construct validity in school violence survey assessment. Items drawn from both the school safety and school climate literature formed the basis of a survey designed specifically to provide a more comprehensive assessment of student perceptions of school safety. Factor analysis of those items yielded four strong factors–Connection/Climate, Incivility and Disruption, Personal Safety, and Delinquency/Major Safety–suggesting that the structure of perceptions of school safety goes well beyond attitudes towards guns, drugs, and gangs. All four factors made strong contributions to the total variance, and high factor loadings and good reliability across all factors indicate a high degree of consistency within each of the empirically derived scales. These results provide empirical validation of theoretical models of school youth violence that stress a comprehensive and preventive focus (Dwyer et al., 1998; Leone et al., 2000; Walker et al., 1996), and in particular models that stress level of student connectedness as a key factor in predicting delinquency and school violence (Hawkins et al., 1998).

Indeed, a number of findings from this investigation converge to suggest that school connection and climate may be *more* critical than delinquency or major safety items in predicting students' overall feelings about the safety of their school in at least some locales. Connection/Climate formed the first factor on the factor analysis, accounting for 28.6% of the total explained variance; in contrast, Delinquency and Major Safety was the last factor extracted, and accounted for only 4% of the explained variance. Even more striking were the results of the regression analysis predicting students' overall perceptions of school safety. Even after accounting for Delinquency and Major Safety, items related to School Connection and Climate resulted in by far the largest change in variance accounted for. Two of the items from the Delinquency/Major Safety factor, *I have seen drugs or alcohol at school* and *Robbery/theft over $10 is common*, that appeared to be significant predictors of overall feelings of safety in step 1 dropped out of the equation when the Connection/Climate items were entered. A number of items stressing school connection (e.g., *Teachers care about me as a person, I am treated fairly at this school*) made significant contributions to overall perceptions of safety. Indeed, of the entire set of items, the item making the single most important contribution to the prediction of overall feelings of safety was, *I feel welcome at this school.* Together, for secondary schools representing rural and suburban areas, these results strongly argue that student perceptions of school safety are influenced less by the criminal violations and physical violence items that predominate on national surveys. Rather students' overall feelings of safety at their school appear to be influenced to a much greater extent by their perceptions of connectedness, climate, and incivility.

Among the more interesting findings were the negative correlations of two academically oriented items (*Teachers work hard to make every student successful* and *Teachers care about student learning*) to overall perceptions of school safety by students. These counterintuitive results are certainly not evidence that school safety and academic achievement are mutually exclusive. But they may indicate that students have a somewhat different perspective on academic accountability and high stakes testing than educators or policy makers. It may well be possible that students in this sample are in agreement with those who have suggested that too intense a focus solely on academic accountability may have deleterious effects on school climate and school bonding (Gordon & Reese, 1997; Osterman, 2000). In general, the relationship between various approaches to achieve improved academic outcomes and school safety has as yet received little research attention, and clearly needs further exploration.

Several limitations of this research should be acknowledged. First, the conditions under which the survey was administered were not consistent across all four sites. In four of the schools, students read the survey from a paper copy and recorded their responses using standard scannable bubble forms. In the fifth, students accessed the survey on the Web from personal computers, recording their responses electronically. Although the surveys contained identical content, it is possible that students' responses were influenced by the mode of presentation. Finally, although our sample was representative of the school context in which the study was situated, it was not racially diverse, and represented only suburban and rural, not urban, locales. It is clear that the absolute values of the descriptive results can in no way be generalized to urban samples. Whether the relationships described in the multivariate analyses hold in more diverse urban school settings remains to be tested. We are currently conducting further analyses in urban schools with moderate to high minority representation to assess the generalizability of the reported factor structure and prediction coefficients.

Furlong and Morrison (1994, 2000) have noted that the study of school violence emerged from fields (e.g., criminal justice) outside of education. The perspective of researchers from those fields appears to have weighted the study of school violence toward an emphasis on criminal violation and physical assault. Increasingly, however, the development of more sophisticated theoretical models of school violence has moved the field toward an awareness of the centrality of school climate and daily disciplinary issues. The current results suggest that serious violent incidents may be less important contributors to perceptions of school safety than perceptions of student connectedness and climate in some school environments. To the extent that these results can be replicated with more diverse samples, they raise concerns about the construct validity of school violence assessment that fails to assess a full continuum of variables that contribute to school violence and its prevention.

NOTE

1. Correlations between overall perceptions of personal safety on the six "I feel safe . . ." items ranged from .548 (I feel safe going to and from school) to .658 (I feel safe in my classrooms). The correlation with the final item in this factor, *I have seen a gun at school this year*, was .264.

REFERENCES

Bruce, A. S., & Desmond, S. A. (1997). Limitations of self-report delinquency surveys: A "hands-on" approach. *Teaching Sociology, 25*, 315-21.

Chandler, K. A., Chapman, C. D., Rand, M. R., & Taylor, B. M. (1998). *Students' reports of school crime: 1989 and 1995.* (NCJRS Document Reproduction Service No. 169607). Washington, DC: Bureau of Justice Statistics, U.S. Department of Justice and National Center for Education Statistics, U.S. Department of Education.

Cornell, D. G., & Loper, A. B. (1998). Assessment of violence and other high-risk behaviors with a school survey. *School Psychology Review, 27*, 317-330.

Cortina, J. M. (1993). What is coefficient alpha? An examination of theory and application. *Journal of Applied Psychology, 78*, 98-104.

Crawford, D., & Bodine, R. (1996). *Conflict resolution education, appendix E: Conflict resolution in schools needs assessment.* Washington, DC: Office of Juvenile Justice and Delinquency Prevention, U.S. Department of Justice.

DeVoe, J. F., Peter, K., Kaufman, P., Ruddy, S. A., Miller, A. K., Planty, M., Snyder, T. D., Duhart, D. T., & Rand, M. R. (2002). *Indicators of school crime and safety: 2002* (NCES 2003-009/NCJ196753). Washington, DC: U.S. Departments of Education and Justice.

Dwyer, K., Osher, D., & Warger, C. (1998). *Early warning, timely response: A guide to safe schools.* Washington, DC: U.S. Department of Education.

Eisenhower, D., Mathiowetz, N. A., & Morganstein, D. (1991). Recall error: Sources and bias reduction techniques. In P. P. Biemer, R. M. Groves, L. E. Lyberg, N. A. Mathiowetz, & S. Sudman (Eds.), *Measurement errors in surveys* (pp. 127-144). New York: Wiley.

Fitzgerald, J. L., & Mulford, H. A. (1986). Self-report validity issues. *Journal of Studies on Alcohol, 48,* 207-211.

Flannery, D. J. (1997). *School violence: Risk preventive intervention and policy.* Urban Diversity Series, no. 109. New York: ERIC Clearinghouse on Urban Education. ERIC Document Reproduction Service No. ED 416 272.

Fox, R. S., Boies, H. E., Brainard, E., Feltcher, E., Huge, J. S., Martin, C. L., Maynard, W., Monasmith, J., Olivero, J., Schmuck, R., Shaheen, T. A., & Stegeman, W. H. (1973). *School climate improvement: A challenge to the school administrator.* Bloomington, IN: Phi Delta Kappa Educational Foundation.

Furlong, M. J., Chung, A., Bates, M., & Morrison, R. L. (1995). Who are the victims of school violence? *Education and Treatment Children, 18,* 1-17.

Furlong, M., & Morrison, G. (1994). Introduction to the miniseries: School violence and safety in perspective. *School Psychology Review, 23,* 139-150.

Furlong, M., & Morrison, G. (2000). The school in school violence: Definitions and facts. *Journal of Emotional & Behavioral Disorders, 8*(2), 71-87.

Gardner, P. L. (1995). Measuring attitudes in sciences: Unidimensionality and internal consistency revisited. *Research in Science Education, 25,* 283-289.

Gordon, S. P., & Reese, M. (1997). High-stakes testing: Worth the price? *Journal of School Leadership, 7*(4), 345-368.

Gottfredson, G. D. (1991). *The Effective School Battery.* Odessa, FL: Psychological Assessment Resources.

Hawkins, J. D., Farrington, D. P., & Catalano, R. F. (1998). Reducing violence through the schools. In D. S. Elliott, B. A. Hamburg, & K. R. Williams (Eds.), *Violence in American schools* (pp. 188-216). New York: Cambridge University Press.

Haynes, N. M., Emmons, C. L., Ben-Avie, M., & Comer, J. P. (1996). *The school development program: Student, staff and parent school climate surveys.* New Haven, CT: Yale Child Study Center.

Heaviside, S., Rowand, C., Williams, C., & Farris, E. (1998). *Violence and discipline problems in U.S. public schools: 1996-97* (NCES 98-030). Washington, DC: U.S. Department of Education, National Center for Education Statistics.

Kann, L., Kinchen, S. A., Williams, B. I., Ross, J. G., Lowry, R., Hill, C. V., Grunbaum, J. A., & Kolge, L. J. (2000). Youth risk behavior surveillance–United States, 1999. *Morbidity and Mortality Weekly Report, 49*(SS-5), 1-94.

Karatzias, A., Power, K. G., & Swanson, V. (2001). Quality of School Life: Development and preliminary standardization of an instrument based on performance indicators in Scottish secondary schools. *School Effectiveness and School Improvement,* *12*(3), 265-284.

Kelly, E. A., Glover, J. A., Keefe, J. W., Halderson, C., Sorenson, C., & Speth, C. (1986). *School Climate Survey (Form A)*. Reston, VA: National Association of Secondary School Principals.

Kingery, P. M., Coggeshall, M. B., & Alford, A. A. (1998). Violence at school: Recent evidence from four national surveys. *Psychology in the Schools,* *35*(3), 247-258.

Larson, J. D. (1994). Violence prevention in the schools: A review of selected programs and procedures. *School Psychology Review,* *23*(2), 151-164.

Lehr, C., & Christenson, S. (2002). Best practices in promoting a positive school climate. In A. Thomas & J. Grimes (Eds.), *Best practices in school psychology IV* (pp. 929-947). Bethesda, MD: The National Association of School Psychologists.

Leone, P. E., Mayer, M. J., Malmgren, K., & Meisel, S. M. (2000). School violence and disruption: Rhetoric, reality, and reasonable balance. *Focus on Exceptional Children,* *33*(1), 1-20.

Lincoln Public Schools. (1998). *Survey of Learning Climate in Elementary Schools.* Lincoln, NE: Author.

McDermott, H. (1998). *Leffler Middle School Safety Survey.* Lincoln, NE: Leffler Middle School, Lincoln Public Schools.

National Association of Secondary School Principals. (1986). *School Climate Survey.* Reston, VA: Author.

National Center for Education Statistics. (1996). *Recommendations of the Crime, Violence, and Discipline Reporting Task Force, NCES 97-581.* Washington, DC: National Education Statistics Agenda Committee.

Newfield, J. (1980). Self reports and matrix sampling: A method of measuring fidelity of implementation. *Studies in Educational Evaluation,* *6*, 149-55.

Opdenakker, M. C., & Van Damme, J. (2000). Effects of schools, teaching staff and classes on achievement and well-being in secondary education: Similarities and differences between school outcomes. *School Effectiveness and School Improvement,* *11*(2), 165-196.

Osterman, K. F. (2000). Students' need for belonging in the school community. *Review of Educational Research,* *70*(3), 323-367.

Resnick, M. D., Bearman, P. S., Blum, R. W., Bauman, K. E., Harris, K. M., Jones, J., Tabor, J., Beuhring, T., Sleving, R. E., Shew, M., Ireland, M., Bearinger, L. H., & Urdy, J. R. (1997). Protecting adolescents from harm: Findings from the National Longitudinal Study on Adolescent Health. *Journal of the American Medical Association,* *278*, 823-832.

Rosenblatt, J. A., & Furlong, M. J. (1997). Assessing the reliability and validity of student self-reports of campus violence. *Journal of Youth and Adolescence,* *26*(2), 187-202.

Shoffner, M. F., & Vacc, N. A. (1999). Psychometric analysis of the Inviting School Safety Survey. *Measurement and Evaluation in Counseling and Development,* *32*, 66-74.

Skiba, R., & Peterson, R. (2003). Teaching the social curriculum: School discipline as instruction. *Preventing School Failure,* *47*(2), 66-73.

Swearer, S. M., & Paulk, D. L. (1998). *The Bully Survey.* Lincoln, NE: Author, University of Nebraska-Lincoln.

Tabachnick, B. G., & Fidell, L. S. (1996). *Using multivariate statistics* (3rd ed.). New York: HarperCollins College Publishers.

U.S. Department of Education. (1998). *Principal/disciplinarian survey on school violence, Fast Response Survey System.* Washington, DC: Author.

U.S. Department of Justice, Bureau of Justice Statistics. (1995). National Crime Victimization Survey: 1995 school crime supplement. Ann Arbor, MI: Interuniversity Consortium for Political and Social Research (ICPSR).

Vossekuil, B., Fein, R., Reddy, M., Borum, R., & Modzeleski, W. (2002). *The final report and findings of the Safe School Initiative: Implications for the prevention of school attacks in the United States.* Washington, DC: U.S. Department of Education and U.S. Secret Service, National Threat Assessment Center.

Walker, H. M., Horner, R. H., Sugai, G., Bullis, M., Sprague, J. R., Bricker, D., & Kaufman, M. J. (1996). Integrated approaches to preventing antisocial behavior patterns among school-age children and youth. *Journal of Emotional and Behavioral Disorders, 4*(4), 194-209.

Index

© 2004 by The Haworth Press, Inc. All rights reserved.

BOOK ORDER FORM!

Order a copy of this book with this form or online at:
http://www.haworthpress.com/store/product.asp?sku=5318

Issues in School Violence Research

___ in softbound at $24.95 (ISBN: 0-7890-2580-9)
___ in hardbound at $49.95 (ISBN: 0-7890-2579-5)

COST OF BOOKS _____

POSTAGE & HANDLING _____
US: $4.00 for first book & $1.50
for each additional book
Outside US: $5.00 for first book
& $2.00 for each additional book.

SUBTOTAL _____
In Canada: add 7% GST. _____

STATE TAX _____
CA, IL, IN, MN, NY, OH & SD residents
please add appropriate local sales tax.

FINAL TOTAL _____
If paying in Canadian funds, convert
using the current exchange rate,
UNESCO coupons welcome.

❑ BILL ME LATER:
Bill-me option is good on US/Canada/
Mexico orders only; not good to jobbers,
wholesalers, or subscription agencies.

❑ Signature _____

❑ Payment Enclosed: $ _____

❑ PLEASE CHARGE TO MY CREDIT CARD:
❑ Visa ❑ MasterCard ❑ AmEx ❑ Discover
❑ Diner's Club ❑ Eurocard ❑ JCB

Account # _____

Exp Date _____

Signature _____
(Prices in US dollars and subject to change without notice.)

PLEASE PRINT ALL INFORMATION OR ATTACH YOUR BUSINESS CARD

Name

Address

City   State/Province   Zip/Postal Code

Country

Tel   Fax

E-Mail

May we use your e-mail address for confirmations and other types of information? ❑ Yes ❑ No We appreciate receiving
your e-mail address. Haworth would like to e-mail special discount offers to you, as a preferred customer.
We will never share, rent, or exchange your e-mail address. We regard such actions as an invasion of your privacy.

Order From Your **Local Bookstore** or Directly From
The Haworth Press, Inc. 10 Alice Street, Binghamton, New York 13904-1580 • USA
Call Our toll-free number (1-800-429-6784) / Outside US/Canada: (607) 722-5857
Fax: 1-800-895-0582 / Outside US/Canada: (607) 771-0012
E-mail your order to us: orders@haworthpress.com

For orders outside US and Canada, you may wish to order through your local
sales representative, distributor, or bookseller.
For information, see http://haworthpress.com/distributors

(Discounts are available for individual orders in US and Canada only; not booksellers/distributors.)

Please photocopy this form for your personal use.
www.HaworthPress.com

BOF04